DECORATIVE P·A·P·E·R

DECORATIVE

P·A·P·E·R

DIANE V. MAURER-MATHISON

WITH JENNIFER PHILIPPOFF • PHOTOGRAPHY BY MICHAEL GRAND

Illustrated
Books

A FRIEDMAN GROUP BOOK

BDD Illustrated Books
An imprint of BDD Promotional Book Company, Inc.
1540 Broadway
New York, N.Y. 10036

BDD Illustrated Books and the accompanying logo are trademarks of the BDD Promotional Book
Company, Inc.

First Published in the United States of America in 1993 by BDD Illustrated Books.

ISBN 0-7924-5839-7

DECORATIVE PAPER
was prepared and produced by
Michael Friedman Publishing Group, Inc.
15 West 26th Street
New York, New York 10010

Editor: Dana Rosen
Art Director: Jeff Batzli
Designer: Tanya Ross-Hughes
Photography Editor: Christopher C. Bain

Typeset by Bookworks Plus
Color separations by United South Sea Graphic Art Co.
Printed in Hong Kong and bound in China by Leefung-Asco Printers Ltd.

Photography © 1993 by Michael Grand
Illustrations © by Jeff Mathison

Dedication

Dedicated to the memory of Anne Vogel and her mother, Anna O'Hearn, whose Irish wit and wisdom still flourish.

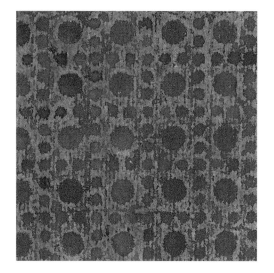

Acknowledgements

Many thanks to all the artists and craftspeople whose exceptional papermaking and paper decorating talents helped shape this book.

CONTENTS

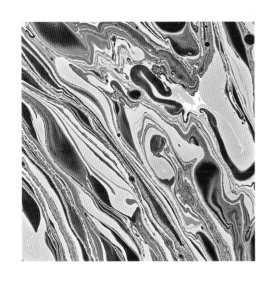

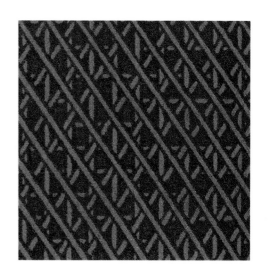

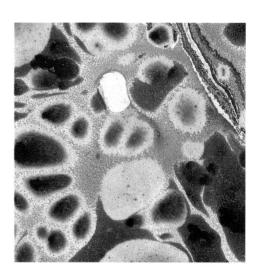

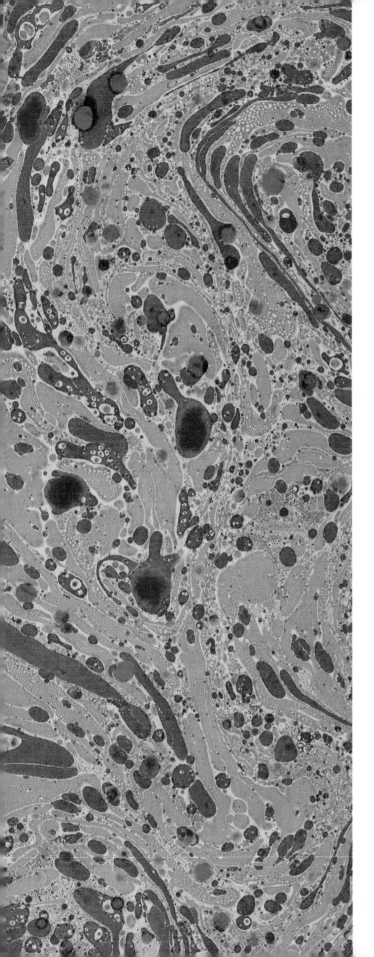

Preface

When I was first asked to write this book, I must admit that I was a bit intimidated by the breadth of the project. Although I was a well-known marbler and produced paste papers professionally, I was only a Sunday papermaker and had limited experience with some of the other paper-decorating media. Oh, I did some pretty far-out tie-dying in the seventies and took a few printmaking workshops some years ago, but I didn't have the expertise I felt I needed to give the work the assured firsthand tone of my other books.

As it turned out, however, I had something more important: a network of friends who were leading papermakers and experienced paper decorators, or who knew others working in the fields I wanted to cover. They were all more than willing to share information and let me show their fine works as excellent models to aspire to. I also had a talented daughter with a strong graphics background who could give life to some of my ideas and illustrate many sections of this book with her own paper designs.

We've taken nothing for granted; we've road-tested every technique conveyed to us and, at times, made discoveries that our advisers have since incorporated into their own works. We've made a few wrong turns, too, but made note of them so you won't have to repeat them.

I worked on the manuscript with some reference books at one end of my desk and a stack of the latest art-supply catalogs at the other. We ordered and tried out many new paper-decorating products available only in recent months. Some proved worthy of passing on to you; others weren't worth their shipping charges.

Wherever possible, I've tried to suggest how to use household or workshop items that you might already have on hand when trying out a medium. Although it's usually true that investing in high-quality art materials will yield the best results, it makes sense to try a craft before purchasing expensive equipment for it. Besides, it's possible to create sophisticated decorative papers with some very low-tech equipment: a potato, for instance.

So, experiment with the various papermaking and paper-decorating techniques and projects in this book, but please use the instructions as guidelines and springboards for your own experiments and ideas. Feel free to break the rules and mix the media. Even the side trips can prove fruitful if you let the spirit of adventure be your guide.

—Diane V. Maurer-Mathison

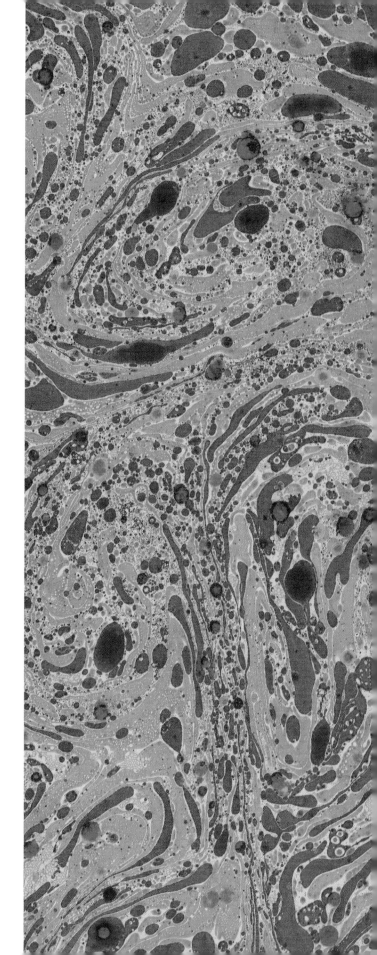

Paper MAKING

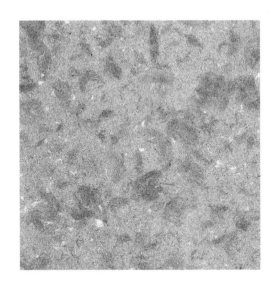

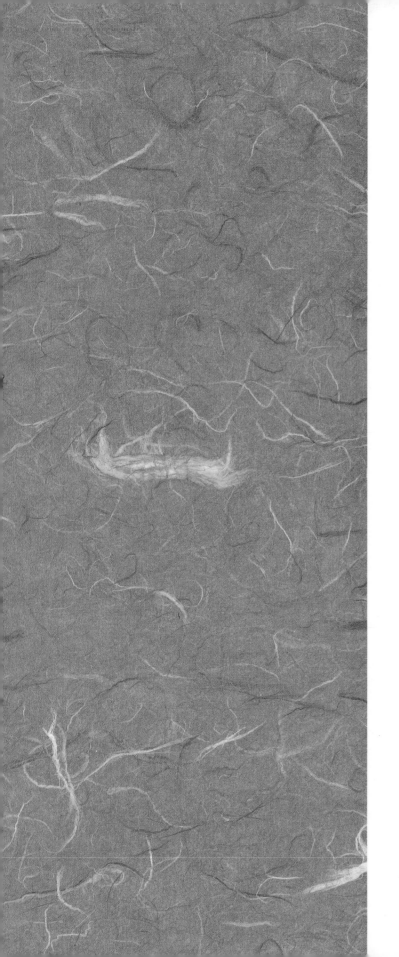

$\mathscr{A}$ Brief History of Papermaking

$\mathscr{I}$t's hard to imagine a world without paper, for we're inundated by it so much in modern times. My mailbox overflows with it daily as the growing waves of mail-order catalogs and advertising circulars arrive. During particularly hectic times, my desk is awash in paperwork. The tasks I try to avoid sink to the bottom of the piles of orders, invoices, and requests for information, only to reappear when the paper shuffling continues. The newspapers pile up, awaiting the recycling bin, and I am convinced that the grocery bags must be reproducing at night.

Still, there are times, especially when I receive an important long-distance phone call, when there's not a scrap of paper in reach. The message pad has been carted off to become a grocery list or a tally sheet for a Scrabble game. I once copied a phone number in some wet clay I was rolling out and on one particularly busy day took brief notes on my wrist. I do stop short of writing on the walls, however. If it's a long message, I usually confess my dilemma to the caller and make him or her wait while I go and search for a pad of paper.

In very early times, of course, before the advent of paper, communicating thoughts by drawing on the walls was considered as right and commonplace as drawing in the sand. Pointed sticks were used to inscribe hieroglyphics on stone, wood, and bark for centuries. Cloth, parchment, and papyrus were also used as writing surfaces, but it wasn't until A.D. 105 that true paper was invented.

Noah Webster defined paper as "a felted sheet of usually vegetable fibers laid down on a fine screen from a water suspension." Dard Hunter, considered to be as much an authority on paper as Mr. Webster was on words, continues:

> To be classified as true paper, the thin sheets must be made from fibre that has been macerated until each individual filament is a separate unit; the fibres intermixed with water, and by the use of a sieve-like screen, the fibres lifted from the water in the form of a thin stratum, the water draining through the small openings of the screen, leaving a sheet of matted fibre upon the screen's surface. This thin layer of intertwined fibre is paper.

So despite the fact that our word *paper* is derived from the word *papyrus,* the laminated stalks of plant material that form papyrus cannot be classified as paper. Likewise, parchment and vellum, because they are made from the skins of animals and are not macerated, are also disqualified.

The ancient Chinese scholars had papyrus, parchment, and woven cloth, which they used to create their calligraphic manuscript scrolls, but the invention of the camel's hair brush in 250 B.C. hastened the development of calligraphy and created a need for a more practical writing surface. Ts'ai Lun is generally credited with providing the solution with his invention of true paper in A.D. 105.

According to Dard Hunter, the idea of making paper was probably a logical outgrowth of the process of cutting and trimming the Chinese cloth scroll. In *Papermaking, the History and Technique of an Ancient Craft*, he theorizes that

> It was probably the narrow strips of waste woven fabric trimmed from the edges of the primeval manuscripts and documents that first suggested to the ever practical Chinese mind the idea of making paper. It is possible that the Chinese conceived the thought of matting and intertwining the fibres into sheets of paper through their knowledge of feltmaking, a craft which antedated even that of weaving.

Some scholars now believe that a kind of paper that was made from silk may have actually predated Ts'ai Lun's paper.

An amazing five hundred years passed before China's closely guarded secret of papermaking techniques was passed on to the artisans of Japan. In Japan, the craft flourished, and many barks and plants were used to make fine paper. Although it is believed that a Buddhist monk was responsible for bringing papermaking to Japan, some Japanese legends maintain that the knowledge was gained from a deity, not a mere mortal. One legend

■ **OPPOSITE PAGE:** *Oriental hand-made papers like this sheet of T-Unryu, which can be found in most art supply stores, can be used for printing and decorative paper projects.*

13

describes a deity disguised as a beautiful woman who appears beside a stream and drapes her kimono over a bamboo stick in imitation of a papermaking mold. According to the legend, the apparition then dipped her supported kimono into a stream and shook it, an action suggesting the formation of a sheet of paper.

The Arabs probably learned the papermaking process from the Chinese in 751, the year of a battle near Samarkand. Apparently some of the Chinese prisoners taken in that battle were experienced papermakers who were forced to divulge secrets. Unlike the Chinese, who were using mulberry bark for papermaking at this time, the Arabs employed linen for papermaking. Various plants or materials indigenous to the areas in which the new craft was introduced were often substituted for the original Chinese papermaking materials: tree bark, old fishnets, and hemp.

The process of reusing cloth fibers sometimes took a bizarre turn. During the twelfth century in Baghdad, some enterprising fellows unwrapped mummies and sold the cloth bands encircling them to paper mills who were creating wrapping paper for the grocers of the day. Again, during the American Civil War, when rags for papermaking were in short supply, some similarly mercenary Americans imported Egyptian mummies to once again make paper for wrapping meat.

It wasn't until the twelfth century, a thousand years after Ts'ai Lun's discovery, that papermaking was introduced into Europe through the Moors. The craft originally surfaced in Xativa, Spain. A hundred years later, the famous Fabriano Mill was built in Italy. By the fifteenth century, France, Germany, and England all had paper mills. And in 1690, the first American paper mill was built in Germantown, Pennsylvania.

As the craft spread, papermakers refined existing techniques and experimented with new materials and techniques for making sheets. The mold on which the matted fibers were created evolved from an Oriental tool probably consisting of four bamboo bars with a flexible mesh of woven grass to the rigid mold and deckle (a second frame used to contain the pulp) favored by Western papermakers today. The wove mold, used in eighteenth-century Europe, was a variation of the rigid laid mold. The wove mold produced a more even sheet of paper without the lines evident in earlier laid papers.

The methods of softening, beating, and macerating the plant and cloth fibers to be made into pulp also varied from place to place; these differing techniques produced papers with various textures, absorbencies, and unique characteristics.

■ *"Key, Pool, Fire" by Helen C. Frederick. The original is a 66- by 28-inch (165 x 70cm) triptych, combining papermaking and monotype printing. Helen draws on a formica surface with water-based crayons and then lays a newly formed sheet of paper over the drawing. As the paper dries, it shrinks and absorbs the drawing into the pulp, producing an image that is both in and on the paper.*

An unfortunate muddy appearance was one of the characteristics of American-made paper prior to the nineteenth century. The unbleached raw materials and discolored water used to create the sheets imparted a cream to dark gray color to the paper. In addition, water dripping from the papermaker's hands often caused semitransparent spots. Specks and spots of various origins, along with hairs from the papermaking felts or from the papermaker's head joined with knotted fibers in many of the older sheets. Occasionally, an insect would fly into the paper pulp. One fifteenth-century piece of paper exists today that, when held to the light, reveals a well-preserved mosquito that had been trapped during the paper formation.

Another type of mark that can be seen in fifteenth-century papers was placed there deliberately. The watermark, a kind of papermaker's signature or trademark, first appeared toward the end of the thirteenth century. An Italian invention, the watermark was usually made from a piece of brass wire, shaped to form a design and stitched with threadlike wires to the papermaking mold. Because the shaped wire was raised from the surface of the mold screen, it left its impression in the wet pulp. The paper was thinner in the area of the watermark and, as a result, showed a translucent design when held to the light.

By the fifteenth century, the watermark was in use throughout Europe. Although it's generally agreed that the original purpose of the watermark was as a kind of trademark, other theories about its origins exist. One theory suggests that besides marking the location of the paper mill, the watermark also showed the quality or size of the paper. Another theory is that watermarks, or "papermarks" as they were called in England, showed religious symbols or signs of secret brotherhoods. Still another explanation is that watermarks were used within the mills as a way to mark the different molds for the illiterate vat men and couchers who often worked in pairs.

These early papermakers worked in damp and unpleasant conditions but had a sense of pride in their work, which demanded a good measure of dexterity and skill. They were hard-pressed to keep up with the increased demands for paper to be used with the new printing machines. When the Fourdrinier papermaking machine was finally perfected in 1810, riots are reported to have taken place outside the mill that housed it. Many papermakers correctly saw that the new machine would be a detriment to their craft. In 1817, the first paper machine in North America was erected near Philadelphia. It did the work of ten vats of the handmade paper mills and produced sheets of great width and seemingly endless length. By the close of the American Civil War, the speed, efficiency, and low cost of the new machine-made paper had made handmade paper obsolete.

Papermaking by hand continued to prosper in the East but barely limped along in most other parts of the world until its recent revival. The renewed interest in papermaking, in Europe, Australia, and North America, is phenomenal. Today it's a much-respected and popular medium for artists and craftspeople who create sheets for bookbinding, fine art, calligraphy, and various forms of paper decorating. Helen C. Frederick and Joe Zina are part of a growing number of people worldwide exploring the limits of the papermaking medium. Their papers are not merely surfaces created to receive art; they *are* the art.

■ *The ROMA watermark identifies this contemporary handmade paper as having been produced at the Fabriano Mill in Italy, which has been in operation since the thirteenth century.*

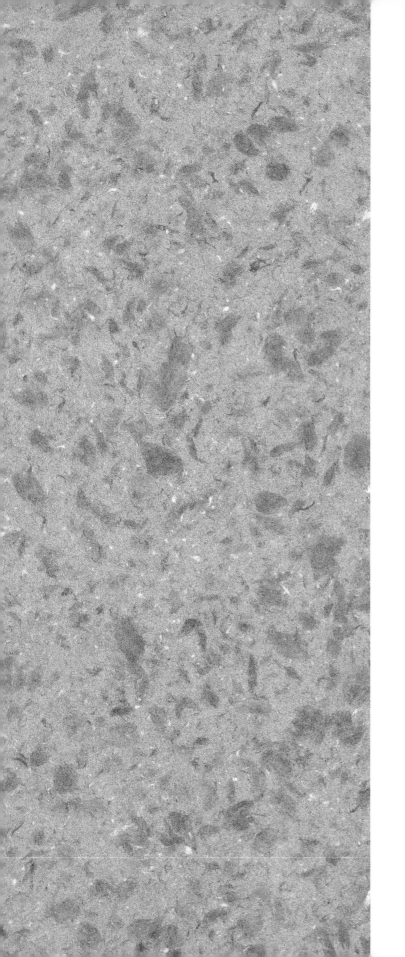

Papermaking

aper can be made from any number of fibrous materials. Wood, linen, banana plant, cotton, mulberry bark, straw, corn stalks, and many other plants all have a high cellulose content, which makes them good for papermaking. When beaten to a pulp and mixed with water, they form a mixture called slurry, which is then poured onto or picked up on a screen, pressed to remove excess moisture, and dried. Through this process, the cellulose material is transformed into handmade paper. The metamorphosis is amazing and the end product quite beautiful. Instead of being used for drawing or paper decoration, these handmade sheets can be appreciated simply for their inherent beauty.

The irregular deckled edges of handmade paper give each sheet a personality and seem to suggest that we've only just barely caught the sheet in that form—it could have gone on to assume any number of shapes.

Although most serious papermakers will eventually look toward purchasing professional equipment such as beaters, molds, and presses, surprisingly good sheets of paper can be produced in your home studio, kitchen, or backyard with a minimum of equipment.

The next section details the equipment and supplies you'll need to begin making paper.

■ OPPOSITE PAGE: *A fantasy paper of multicolored pulp created by Rugg Road Papers and Prints. The original size is 18 by 24 inches (45 x 60cm).* **ABOVE:** *"A Rush of Pink" by Jeanne Petrosky. Image size is 6 by 2¾ inches (15 x 7cm). Jeanne layers and manipulates the deckled edges of her handmade papers to form delicate relief sculptures.*

■ EQUIPMENT AND MATERIALS

Papermaking is a wonderfully wet and messy process; I recommend working outside if at all possible. A garage or basement with a concrete floor would also be a good choice to use as a papermaking studio, as long as you observe safety precautions.

*E*QUIPMENT

- A kitchen blender.
- A 32-ounce (1L) measuring cup.
- A large sponge.
- A plastic dishpan or other large pan to serve as the papermaking vat. A busboy's tub, which can be purchased at a restaurant supply store, is ideal for larger sheets of paper.
- Several pieces of old cotton sheets, all-purpose dishcloths (Handiwipes), or dressmaker's interfacing, slightly larger than the papers you plan to make, to use as supportive couching cloths.
- Nonrusting pushpins.
- A large sheet of Styrofoam or waterproofed plywood to which you will pin papers.
- Plastic sheeting to protect the table and floor if you don't want them to get wet.
- A plastic apron to protect the papermaker.

Mold

The last piece of equipment you'll need for your first foray into papermaking is some sort of mold. To make a simple one, staple some fiberglass window screening to a waterproofed wooden frame about 8 by 10 inches (20 x 25cm) wide. A larger mold can be made if it will fit into your papermaking vat and still give you room to maneuver.

An old picture frame or small painting stretcher will also do. You can also sandwich the mesh between the sections of an embroidery hoop to create a simple round mold. If necessary, run duct tape over the edges of the screen to hold it in place; the screen should be good and tight.

*M*ATERIALS

You can order cotton or abaca linters (pulp in sheet form) from a papermaking supply house. Simply tear these up and mix them with water to form a strong pulp. You can also recycle computer paper; old blotters; paper egg cartons; and pieces of drawing, typing, or printmaking paper. Some people are delighted to be able to recycle old newspapers into handmade paper, but you should be aware that newsprint will produce a weak paper. The quality of your handmade sheet will be only as good as the quality of the material from which it's made. If you want your sheets to be strong and lasting, it's best to shy away from using tissues, paper towels, newsprint, and paper with high wood pulp or an acid content.

In addition, use purified water or distilled water if you're concerned about paper life. Small brown foxing spots can eventually appear on paper that was made from water that contained iron, copper, or manganese.

■

BASIC PAPERMAKING

𝒫REPARING THE PULP

Cut or tear a quantity of your papermaking material into 1- to 2-inch (2.5–5cm) pieces and let them soak in water overnight. You can also boil the raw material, called the furnish, to speed up the process of breaking down the fibers. If you're using linters, little preparation is necessary; you'll only need to dampen and tear them immediately before pulping.

When the fibers are ready, add a small handful of your materials (about a 4-inch [10cm] square of linters) to a blender two-thirds full of warm water. A general rule is to add about one part pulp to two parts warm water. Beat the mixture by adding the furnish a little at a time and blending it for about a minute. Use short bursts of speed to avoid taxing the motor. The pulp fibers should eventually be suspended cloudlike in the liquid without showing knots of pulp. Pour some of the pulp and water into a small glass to check for the proper consistency. When the pulp is smooth and free of clumps, pour it into your vat and add at least two more blendersful of water. Continue until you have a mixture of about 1 pint (500ml) of concentrated pulp to 4 gallons (15L) of water. For thick sheets of paper you'll want a high concentration of pulp to water. For thin sheets you'll want your pulp more diluted. Eventually you'll learn to judge how thick to make the pulp for the particular paper you desire.

𝒻ORMING THE FIRST SHEET

Stir the water and suspended pulp with your hand until it is evenly mixed and then scoop up some of the pulp mixture in your measuring cup. Hold your mold over the pan and pour the pulp mixture as evenly as possible over the flat, but not recessed area of your mold. Repeat the procedure until you have about ⅛ inch (3mm) of pulp sitting on top of the screen.

Let the pulp drain for a moment and then invert the mold onto a dampened piece of cloth to couch (rhymes with pooch) the sheet. When the paper pulp is completely sandwiched between the cloth and the mold, take a damp sponge and press the pulp onto the cloth, or felt, through the back of the screen. This will press out some of the excess water and also help release the paper from the screen.

Wring out the sponge and press it against the back of the screen until it again becomes saturated. When your sponge-pressed sheet has released itself from the screen, pin the cloth it's resting on to the Styrofoam or wood drying board, and let the paper air-dry. If the couching cloth is pinned tautly, the adhering paper won't shrink very much as it dries.

2-1

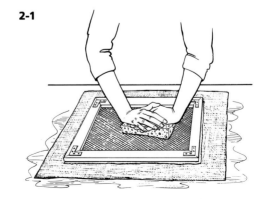

■ **FIGURE 2-1.** *Pressing the excess water from a newly couched sheet of paper helps to release it from the mold.*

■ **FIGURE 2-2.** *You can use small picture frames or canvas stretchers to make the frames for your mold and deckle, or you can construct them with strips of wood. Square or mitered corners are both fine as long as you make sure the corner joints are tightly screwed or nailed. Reinforce them with nonrusting corner braces. To make your mold, stretch brass, aluminum, or fabric mesh screening over your mold frame. Keep the mesh as taut as possible and secure it with brass tacks or copper staples.*

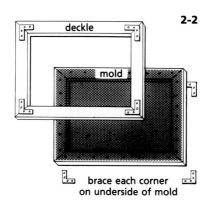

2-2

deckle

mold

brace each corner
on underside of mold

■ **FIGURE 2-3.** *Dip your mold into the papermaking vat at a 45-degree angle to begin scooping up the suspended pulp.*

This crude version of unsized, or waterleaf, paper will satisfy many young people and tentative papermakers eager to get a taste of simple papermaking. Sheets formed this way are fine for collages and many similar uses, but they won't be as strong or as evenly formed as the papers you can make with a bit more equipment and involvement on your part.

■

REFINING YOUR PAPERMAKING: USING A MOLD AND DECKLE

Now that your appetite for papermaking has been whetted, you will want to add a well-built mold and deckle to your equipment list. You may also want to add some papermaking felts that were either purchased or cut from old woolen army or baby blankets to your supply of couching cloths. These will be especially important if you want to make what's known as a post of several sheets of paper and press them at the same time.

You can purchase felts and equipment such as paper presses and molds with companion deckles from papermaking supply houses. You can also construct this equipment yourself using the plans shown in figure 2-2. The mold should be made of waterproofed wood with nonrusting hardware so that it won't be harmed by repeated exposure to water. The deckle, or frame that is placed on top of the mold to help contain the pulp, will also be waterproofed. This new piece of equipment, which will have the same dimensions as the mold, gives the sheet its deckled edges. An important piece of

equipment, the deckle is used when forming a sheet of paper by dipping into a vat of suspended pulp.

FORMING A SHEET OF PAPER BY DIPPING INTO THE VAT

To make a well-formed sheet of paper using your mold and deckle, first agitate your pulp/water slurry and then place your deckle on top of your mold so that the flat edges are together. Hold the deckle in place with your thumbs and grasp the mold with your fingers.

Next dip the bottom edge of your mold and deckle into the vat at the far edge. Hold it at about a 45-degree angle and bring it toward you, holding it level for a moment just below the surface of the pulp. Then bring it swiftly up and out of the vat. A layer of pulp will come with it, its edges contained by the deckle. As the water drains through the mesh screen, gently shake the mold forward and back and from side to side to help the paper fibers to mesh. This slight shifting action, sometimes called "throwing off the wave," helps form a strong sheet of paper. Next, tilt the mold and deckle slightly to allow some of the excess water to drain off into the vat.

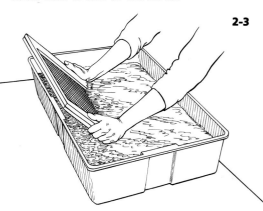

2-3

If your first efforts are a bit ragged and unsuccessful, or in historic tradition, you've dripped water onto your pulp-covered screen, causing holes to appear in your paper, you can also "throw off" or "kiss off" the sheet, to use the papermakers' terms. To do this, remove the deckle and place the mold facedown on the water surface. The pulp will release itself and join the pulp mixture again.

If your paper is too thin, add more blended pulp to the mixture in the vat; if it's too thick, add more water.

$\mathcal{C}$OUCHING

When you have a satisfactory layer of pulp resting on the mold, remove the deckle and couch the sheet. This time, let the mold stand upright at the right edge of the felt, and roll it firmly down. As the left edge of the mold makes contact with the felt, lift the right edge up. Usually the slight rocking motion made by these actions will release the sheet of newly formed paper, making sponging the back of the sheet unnecessary.

2-4

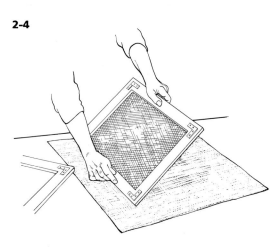

You can couch the paper onto a wet cloth and air-dry it as before, or couch it onto a piece of Formica covered with a wet blanket or felt. If you alternate sheets of paper and felts, you can build up a post, or stack, of papers. Then, if you add a Formica cover board to the post of papers you can press out moisture from all the papers at the same time. Instructions for making a simple press are shown in figure 2-5.

2-5

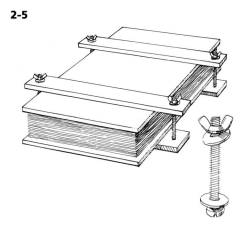

$\mathcal{D}$RYING

Sheets that have been sponged or pressed to remove most of the moisture can be air-dried to retain texture, or placed between dry cloths or blotters and ironed to impart a smooth surface.

Another method of drying a newly couched sheet is to place it facedown on a piece of Formica and, using a wide brush, firmly brush the couching cloth and paper against the Formica. Finally, peel away the cloth and let the paper, now adhering to the Formica, air-dry. When the sheet is dry, you can peel it off the Formica and one side of the paper will be quite smooth and flat.

■ **FIGURE 2-5.** *In this simple version of a paper press, strips of water-proofed wood and bolts with wing nuts apply pressure to formica boards that encase the wet paper stack.*

■ **FIGURE 2-4.** *To couch your sheet of paper, let the mold stand upright on your felt or couching cloth and then lower the edge of the mold so your pulp makes contact with the felt.*

■

PAPERMAKING TECHNIQUES

𝒰SING RAW PLANT MATERIAL TO FORM A PULP

It's fairly easy to dry and add bits of seeds, leaves, and petals to your abaca or cotton linters before forming a sheet of paper, but using raw plant material as a base for your pulp can be a bit more involved. Some plant materials are so tough that they must be pounded and then chopped into fine pieces or well shredded to get them ready for processing. The fleshy parts of plants are usually removed by boiling them in a stainless steel or enamel pot for several hours; a caustic solution is sometimes added to help break down the fibers, but boiling them for a day or so will usually achieve the same results. (Limited experiments seem to suggest that a micro-

wave can speed things up.) The brackish water resulting from the first cooking is usually removed, and fresh water is added to the plant material before it gets cooked for another length of time. When it's quite mushy and slippery, the plant material is mixed with water and beaten to form a pulp.

The Japanese are masters at forming exotic papers from a variety of plants, including *kozo, gampi,* and *mitsumata.* Some of the many books devoted entirely to papermaking using raw plant materials and Oriental techniques are listed in the bibliography. To get a feel for papermaking using found plants, experiment with the following as additives to linter pulp or as a base for the pulp: gladiola leaves, onion skins, pampas grass, cattails, hay, wheat, straw, and cabbage stumps. Try using your own garden plants, too. A word of caution, however: be sure that the plant you cook is nontoxic. I know firsthand how important this advice is, having gotten quite sick one day while cooking a lovely plant that turned out to be deadly oleander.

𝒲ATERMARKS

Watermarks, the translucent symbols often seen in the corners of handmade paper, are a kind of signature of the papermaker or paper mill. These symbols are usually created with a piece of brass wire bent into a design and sewn into the mold screen. When the pulp spreads over the surface of the mold, the wire displaces some of the pulp, causing the paper to be thinner in that area. When the sheet dries, the image of the wire becomes visible as the watermark.

■ *Highly textured, but very fragile papers can be made with onion skins and lawn clippings.*

You can shape and attach thin brass wire or monofilament line to make your own unique watermark. Some papermakers also draw their watermark on the mold with waterproof glue.

*A*DDING TEXTURE

Tooth, or texture, can be added to a sheet of paper by couching onto a textured cloth. Lace tablecloths, cheesecloth, or doilies can all be used. Pieces of lace can also be placed between the damp paper and a cloth or blotter before it's ironed to emboss the surface of the paper as it dries. I made a delightful little sheet of paper this way using pieces of antique lace. The surface of the ironed sheet bore the distinct impression of the satin roping. The reverse side of the paper, however, turned out even more interesting; the antique dyes were not colorfast and where the lace made contact with the wet pulp it left a lovely dyed depression.

Embossing can also be accomplished by laying objects on the couched sheet before it's put in the press. Air-dried sheets, too, can be embossed by pressing objects onto them and letting the objects dry in the paper. Corrugated cardboard, pieces of wire, string, fish skeletons, and even glass rods pushed into the sheets can make a good impression. Be aware of the fact that some unprotected metals can leave rust stains on your papers, however. In one instance, I was enjoying trapping the impression of a small pair of scissors in one of my papers until I noticed strange brown rust stains appearing in the sheet. An unusual way to color a sheet, perhaps, but nothing I'd care to repeat in the future.

*A*DDING TEXTURE TO THE PULP

Bits of milkweed, coconut hairs, corn silk, glitter, and various seeds and spices can be added to the slurry just before the sheet is formed. Dried flower petals and onion skins often lend texture and color, and immortalizing a blossom in a piece of handmade paper is a nice way to preserve a favorite plant or gift bouquet. I find that microwaving most blossoms will dry them in about three minutes with very little color loss; this is a good technique to use when summer rains make flower drying difficult.

■ *Antique lace and scissors left their impressions and some unexpected color in two of my handmade papers (**top and bottom**). Japanese lace paper is famous for its delicate patterns and textures (**background**).*

*E*MBEDDING MATERIALS IN THE PULP

Leaves, dried flowers, gold stars, colored cellophane, bits of colored thread, feathers, and even pieces of other decorative papers can be pressed into a newly formed sheet and partially covered with a wispy film of pulp to help them adhere. Use a spoon or turkey baster to deposit the watery pulp. Or try couching an almost transparently thin piece of paper over the previously couched piece.

Bits of dried material, mica particles, and tiny pieces of paper will sometimes adhere of their own accord if they're sprinkled on a very wet sheet. An eccentric friend of mine once created a paper by sprinkling tiny confetti-sized letters over a newly couched sheet. Iridescent accents next to the letters came from a surprising source—they were the eyes of dead flies he'd been collecting from his light fixtures all summer long!

Another papermaker experimented by embedding alfalfa seeds between two couched sheets. They were kept in the dark for a while and eventually sprouted to unveil themselves as a living (and eventually dying) piece of art.

*A*LTERING THE SHEET

Another way to create texture in a sheet of hand-made paper is to remove parts of the pulp while it is on the mold. To create a lacy effect, intentionally squirt or drop water onto the uncouched sheet. In the areas where the water hits, the pulp will be pushed aside and a hole will be formed.

Tearing a sheet by pulling on a string embedded in the couched paper can lead to interesting distortions. You can tear the sheet while it is still in a damp state or wait until it's fully dry to give it a unique character. If you tear slowly you can often control the angle and degree of distortion.

■ *Microwaved peony petals were added to paper pulp to form this flower paper (**left**). Bits of ribbon, some confetti, and wisps of thread help embellish this "Rugg Road Special" handmade paper (**right**).*

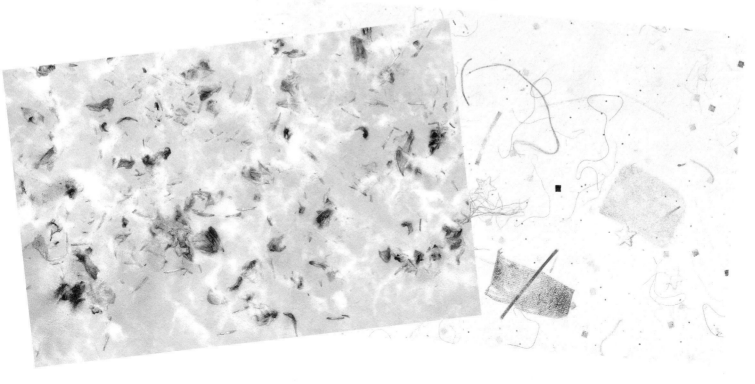

You can also alter a sheet by allowing only part of your mold to enter the slurry and letting some of the pulp drip down your screen instead of having the pulp totally cover it.

DYEING THE PULP

Because the paper pulp is made of natural fibers, a number of dyes used to color cotton or linen cloth can be used to color paper. Natural dyes and inks, Rit dye, acrylic paints, and Procion and Pientex can all be mixed into your pulp. Some colors may fade more than others, and some will lend a darker tint. Acrylics tend to dry to a paler color than some of the other coloring agents. Adding colored paper to your pulp is another way to give a slight tint. A papermaking supplier can provide you with high-quality dyes in an assortment of colors and intensities. Combining various colored pulps in the vat can produce interesting multicolored flecked sheets.

LAMINATING

Couching a very thin sheet of paper over another to glue embedded objects down is a form of laminating. Because wet pulp will adhere to wet pulp, all kinds of images can be formed by couching sheets or strips of paper to each other.

To laminate, couch your first sheet of paper and allow it to stand quite wet and unpressed. Allowing the first sheet to remain wet is necessary to permit the second sheet to adhere properly. When your second sheet is formed, couch it on top of the first sheet, then press the sheets together as one.

If the second sheet is couched directly on top of the first, a thicker sheet of paper will be formed. You can also use the laminating process to create a wider sheet of paper by couching the second sheet of paper beside the first while allowing the edges to overlap. Couching a second or third sheet off-center will lead to the formation of free-form sheets, no longer bearing the mold's shape. You can, of course, also vary the colors of the laminated areas to create a multicolored piece of paper.

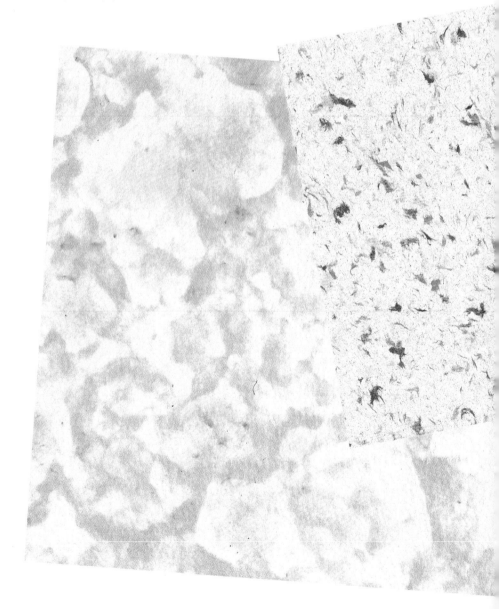

■ *Swirls of dyed pulp create the cloudlike appearance of the "Pulp Marble" sheets by David Carruthers of the Saint Armand Paper Mill (**far left and right**). A "Rugg Road Special" of multicolored pulp (**left center**). A Saint Armand marsh grass paper (**right center**).*

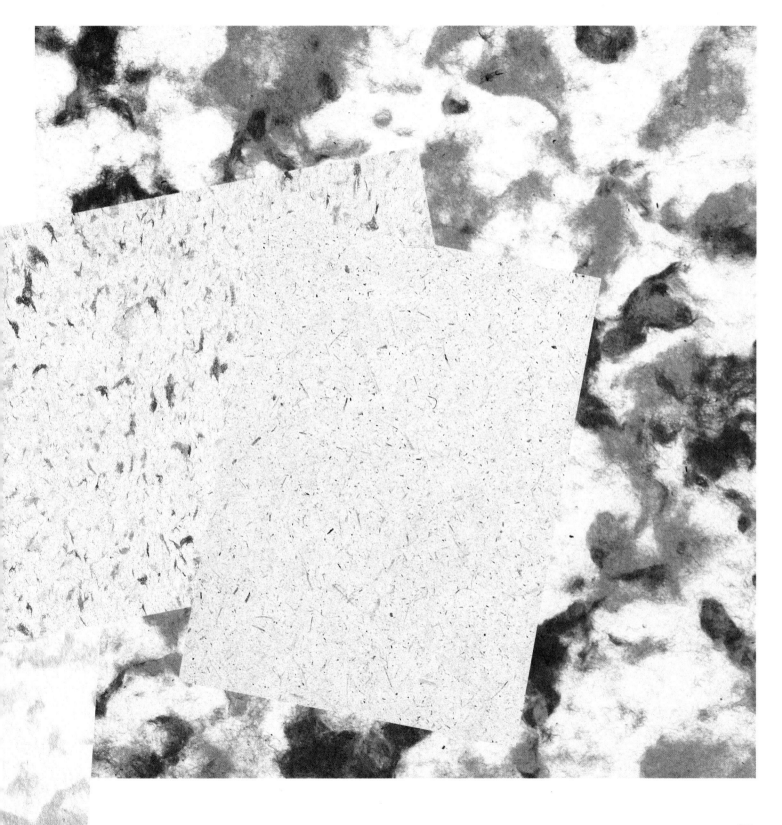

Masking Off Parts Of Your Mold

You can create narrow strips of paper by closing off parts of your mold's screen with lines of masking tape. When you bring your mold up out of the vat, the water will drain through the unmasked mesh screen and allow the pulp fibers in that area to join. The pulp sitting on top of the lines of masking tape will come off when you peel the tape back. Any remaining wayward pulp can be picked off with your fingers.

You can create a row of stripes this way by laminating straight across or diagonally across another sheet of paper. A second row of stripes can be couched over the first to create a grid. By varying the length, placement, and color of narrow strips of pulp, complexly patterned papers can be created.

Contact paper can be placed on your screen to mask out parts of it, too. We like to use several

molds with areas permanently masked out to allow us to easily produce shaped papers. The folio pictured on this page was created on a masked-off screen that's been used many times.

If you don't want to bother making a new mold or risk blocking your screen with contact-paper residue, mask out an extra piece of fiberglass screen that just fits inside your deckle. If your mold is relatively small, this second screen will work quite well.

■ **ABOVE:** *This lovely sheet comprised of diagonally laminated strips of paper was created by Joe Zina. The original sheet is 12 by 18 inches (30 x 45cm).* **LEFT:** *The folio produced on our masked-off screen holds a number of 4- by 6-inch (10 x 15cm) hand-made sheets.*

Altering Your Mold With Templates

By holding a template against the surface of your mold and dipping into your vat, you can create a number of uniquely shaped papers. The pulp will fill in the open areas of your template or stencil. It can then be couched onto a differently colored wet sheet

■ *"Cartoon Jungle" by Joe Zina. This pulp painting consisting of three panels measures 40 by 83 inches (100 x 208cm). Leaves made of preformed paper were added to the painting after it dried.*

or simply couched onto a felt to become a pig-, moon-, or star-shaped piece of paper.

If you cut the template out of masonite or waterproofed plywood, it can become a permanent part of your papermaking equipment. Foam core can be used a number of times before it begins to break down, and mat board can be used in a pinch. Both of these materials can be waterproofed by covering them with clear contact paper before cutting them.

An easy way to make a stencil or template from a magazine illustration is to sandwich a piece of carbon paper between the image you want to reproduce and the stencil material. Then you can just trace the outline of the shape and transfer the drawing to the waterproofed foam core. It is easier to reproduce curved shapes in pulp. If your template contains an

intricate shape with sharp angles, it will be difficult to remove it without tearing the enclosed pulp.

PAINTING WITH PULP

Extra-thin slurry can be made by watering down some of the pulp in your vat; if you then transfer this to a turkey baster or plastic squeeze bottle you can draw or paint with the pulp. Snip off the tip of the bottle, if necessary, to get the pulp to flow correctly. Colored pulp can be squirted onto a wet couched sheet in a controlled or an artfully haphazard way to add interest to a piece of handmade paper. You might also try drawing or lettering with the pulp directly on the mold and then couching onto another sheet.

■ *A dinosaur-shaped candy mold and several torn sheets of handmade paper were used to create this novel card.*

Casting with Pulp

Very thick pulp can be pressed into a mold to create a relief form. The dinosaur pictured on this page was made by simply pressing pulp into a plastic candy mold. Butter and cookie molds or found objects such as shells can also be used. Different-colored pulps can be mixed in the mold, or objects can be embedded in the paper by placing them in the mold before applying the pulp.

Apply the wet pulp by pressing it into the mold with a sponge, felting the paper as you work. If you keep wringing out the sponge you can remove most of the water and speed up drying time. When the cast pulp is completely dry, gently peel it from the mold. If your mold doesn't release cleanly, spray it with a vegetable oil or plastic spray before applying the pulp.

Plaster molds can also be made by forming a relief work in modeling clay and pouring plaster over it. When the plaster hardens, it assumes the shape of the clay. When the clay is removed, a recessed form is left, which if coated with shellac, can be repeatedly used as a casting mold. Care must be taken to create a form without undercuts, however, to prevent wet pulp from entering these recessed areas and anchoring the dried cast piece so that it can't be removed from the mold.

Cast papers can take days to dry. Let them dry outdoors in the sunlight or use a hair dryer to speed up the process.

■ ABOVE: *This flower sculpture by Jean Giddings consists of four separate sections that nest inside each other. It is 16 inches (40cm) in diameter and 7 inches (18cm) deep.* **RIGHT:** *"Pond" by Diane Maurer-Mathison. This relief sculpture of handmade paper, with suminagashi marbling and dried grass, is 17 by 12½ inches (43 x 31cm).*

Casting with a Sheet of Paper

Couched sheets that have been sponged to remove some of the excess water can be laid into or over a shaped mold and pressed with a sponge, bone folder, or other smooth implement to ease them into a shape. Rubber snakes, antique brooches, and various other relief forms can all be used as molds. Or you can create a form out of modeling clay and lay a couched sheet over that. The lily pods in "Pond" were made by casting over balls of clay.

One of the advantages of sheet casting is that you can make your paper conform to either the interior or the exterior structure of the forms you choose. Jean Giddings' delicate flower sculptures take their shapes from both the convex and the concave shapes of glass and ceramic bowls.

■

FINAL STEPS

Sizing

Because handmade paper is naturally absorbent, certain types of paints and inks will feather, or bleed, into the paper when they're applied. In many cases, this enhances a work. But if you want to use your paper for stationery and don't plan to use a ballpoint pen, or if you need a nonabsorbent paper, you'll want to add some sort of sizing to your sheets. Papermaking suppliers sell an internal sizing that is added to the pulp when it's being beaten.

Paper may also be externally or surface-sized by spraying a dried sheet with a mixture of powdered starch and water. Mix about ½ teaspoon (2ml) of starch with 1 pint (0.5L) of water and transfer to a plant mister to size papers. Acrylic spray mediums can also be sprayed on sheets to size them.

Cleaning Up

Any pulp that's left in your vat after your papermaking session should be strained out and refrigerated for use within a few days. You can also compress and freeze balls of pulp or let them dry out, then rehydrate and remix them months later. To avoid clogging drains, strain all pulp liquid as it's being poured down the sink. Hose off your molds and deckles and brush off your felts to prevent dried pulp from interfering with future papermaking.

Paper DECORATING

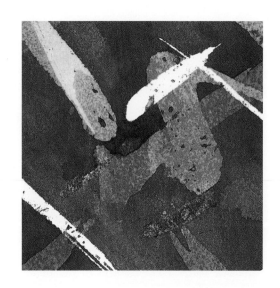

A Brief History of Paper Decorating

*S*oon after humans learned to make marks on paper to communicate thoughts and ideas, they began to make marks for decorative purposes. Drawings, no doubt, came first, but allover patterns soon followed. As early as the fifth century, the Chinese engraved seals in wood, jade, horn, and bamboo, coated them with ink, and used them to stamp paper. By the seventh century, they were experimenting with stencils and paper cutting. An early form of paper marbling, Suminagashi, was practiced in Japan in the twelfth century and possibly even earlier in China. By the sixteenth century, complicated fine-combed marbling, which originated in Persia, had been introduced into many European countries. At the same time, incised and stamped colored paste was being used to decorate papers in Germany, France, and Italy. By the eighteenth-century, paper decorating was flourishing in North America, as well as in Europe. Wood-block repeat and embossed patterns graced many a sheet of paper.

Some of the decorative sheets were used as wrapping papers or for lining drawers or boxes. The poorer folk, especially in France, used woodblock-patterned papers as a substitute for the

■ **OPPOSITE PAGE:** *Oil marbling on carrageenan size by Paul Maurer. The original sheet size is 11 by 17 inches (28 x 43cm).* **ABOVE:** *"Telling Time in Heaven" by Tom West. This 8¾- by 4¼- by 15½-inch (22 x 11 x 39cm) working clock is decorated with paste and ebru- and suminagashi-marbled papers. It is constructed of wood, cardboard, acrylic paints, and metallic leaf.* **RIGHT:** *"Twilight Mesa" by Diane Maurer-Mathison. This 15-inch (38cm) square collage incorporates oil marbling, handmade paper, and pulled-paste techniques.*

textile wall hangings popular with their more well-to-do counterparts. In the days before papermaking machines made rolls of wallpaper possible, a single sheet of decorated paper was often prized as a means of livening up a drab wall.

During the eighteenth century, decorated papers bearing tiny patterns were often produced for a particular purpose. In her much-respected work *Decorated Book Papers*, Rosamond B. Loring notes:

> Black and white papers were made for funeral notices, checkered papers for the tops of chessboards. Others were used for the backs of playing cards or in the form of colored sheets in small designs for the game of lotto. Boxes and cupboards of all sorts were lined with them; they were used for covering the backs of mirrors; small pamphlets and almanacs were bound in them. They were used in France, Italy, Germany, and England both for book covers and for end-papers all through the eighteenth century.

Sadly, when the binding process became mechanized, many hand-decorating techniques were deemed too slow to be commercially feasible. As machine-printed papers became more and more sought after, many of the hand-decorating processes went out of vogue.

The resurgence of the crafts movement and the growing respect for the handmade have fostered a new interest in various forms of paper decorating. Many of the "lost arts," such as marbling and paste papermaking, are being rediscovered. Paper decorating extends well beyond the realm of book arts today. Its various techniques are being used by designers and decorators to produce distinctive home furnishings ranging from large room dividers to miniature treasure boxes.

Advertising agencies and publishing companies are using a wide range of decorative papers for their striking visual impact. Book jackets and mail-order circulars often show the mark of the craftsperson. Even television stations sometimes use a muted decorative design as a backdrop for their station identification spots.

Many patterned papers can stand on their own, of course, and transcend being decorative designs used to embellish objects or showcase products. In the hands of an artist like Tom West, hand-printed papers often become integral parts of constructions like "Telling Time in Heaven." Paper-decorating techniques can also be combined to produce works like "Twilight Mesa," which I created by using paste techniques over a marbled image.

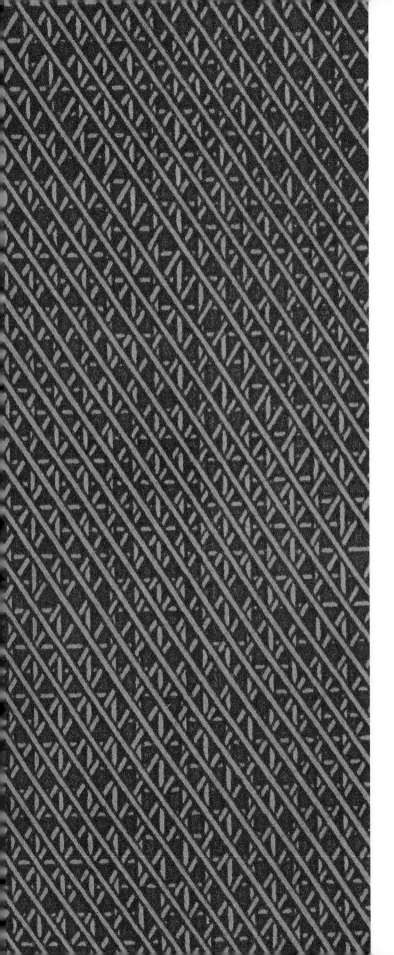

C H A P T E R   4

aste Papers

$\mathcal{P}$aste papers are made by brushing paste on a dampened sheet of paper, and creating patterns by displacing the paste with any number of tools or found objects. Fingers can be used, too, for a kind of finger painting. It's easy to make pleasing images with little skill, and any child can be entertained for hours drawing in paste. Like most crafts, however, in the hands of a professional or a novice who is sensitive to graphic images, the medium can yield sophisticated and complicated results.

The precision and delicacy of Claire Maziarczyk's papers and the bold, contemporary three-dimensionality of the papers made by Nora Ligorano and Virginia Buchan show the wide range of images that can be achieved with this medium. These professionals, who have spent years exploring paste papers, give us all something to aspire to. The next section will tell you what you need to begin working with paste paper.

■

EQUIPMENT AND MATERIALS

- A shallow pan or nearby sink to wet your paper in.
- 2-quart (2L) saucepan.
- Measuring cup and spoons.
- 2 sponges.
- A small paintbrush for mixing color into the paste.
- Large 3- to 4-inch (8–10cm) high-quality paintbrushes for applying paste (one for each color used).
- Strainer (in case the paste is lumpy).
- A sheet of Plexiglas or Formica to work on. An old enamel tabletop or a wooden table covered with plastic can also serve as a working surface.
- A folding clothes rack or drying line.
- Wide, flat containers with covers for holding the colored paste. Food-storage containers with lids are ideal, as long as they're big enough to accommodate your paste brushes. Cat food or tuna cans can be used for an afternoon of paste adventures.

Patterning Tools

A number of different tools can be used for making patterns in paste. For combed paste papers, plastic hair picks and multiple-line calligraphy pens of all sizes make interesting marks. Plastic forks, pastry wheels, wood-graining combs, and potters' tools also lend themselves to the medium. You can make combs from milk or soda bottles by cutting out sections of flat plastic and using an X-Acto knife or scissors to create various-sized teeth. Pinking shears can also be used to create a serrated edge on a piece of plastic.

Incised corks, rolling pins with decorative designs cut into them, buttons, nuts, and bottle tops are just a few of the hundreds of objects that you can use to create a repeating stamped pattern in paste. Stamping can be done in conjunction with combed areas or by itself on a sheet. Even slapping a 2-inch (5cm) paintbrush against a pasted sheet at regular intervals can produce interesting designs.

Paper

A 70-pound (31.5kg) offset printing paper is ideal for making paste papers. Canson Mi-Teintes, Strathmore, and many other drawing papers also give good results. The paper must be strong enough to withstand being wet and having tools drawn across its surface in a pasted and dampened state. Highly absorbent papers should be avoided, as they usually tend to shred as you work them.

Color

Various types of colors can be used to make paste papers. Poster paints, tube gouache, watercolor paint, and acrylics all work fine. You might want to buy just the three primary colors, red, blue, and yellow, and then mix them to create a more extensive palette.

■ **OPPOSITE PAGE:** *"Red Cross Hatch" by Claire Maziarczyk. The original is 19 by 25 inches (48 x 63cm).* **RIGHT:** *An extensive color palette can be obtained by color mixing. Twelve hues can be created using the primary colors: red, yellow, and blue. Primary, secondary, and tertiary colors can be further altered by tinting with white or shading with black.*

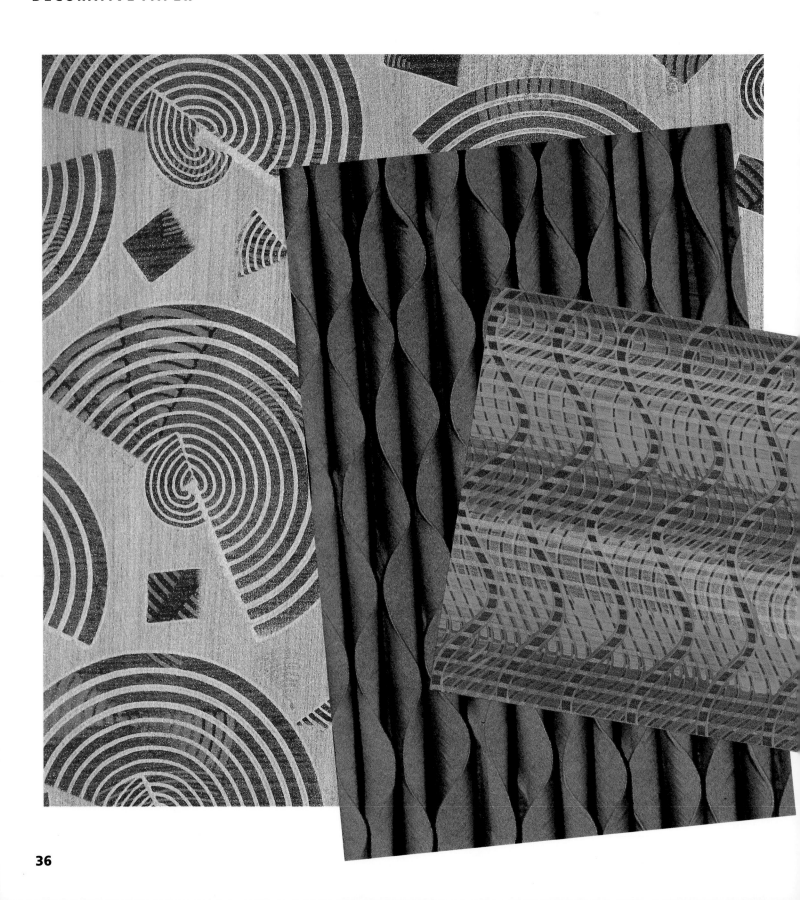

■ **OPPOSITE PAGE:** *These striking graphic images are details from the paste papers of Nora Ligorano and Virginia Buchan (**left and center**) and Claire Maziarczyk (**right**). The papers on the left and right show multiple-image designs made by patterning paste that had been applied over a previously finished sheet. Actual paper size is 25 by 38 inches (63 x 95cm).*

■

MAKING, COLORING, AND APPLYING THE PASTE

Every paste-paper maker has a favorite recipe, and most work about equally well. Some people swear by rice flour or a mixture of rice and wheat flour. The following formulas have been developed by us; feel free to experiment, adding more flour to thicken the paste or more water to dilute your mixture if it becomes too stiff. As in making gravy, if you stir the flour with a little water to dilute it and continue to stir while adding additional liquid, you shouldn't wind up with troublesome lumps to strain out.

𝓕LOUR PASTE RECIPE

4 tablespoons (60ml) rice flour

3 tablespoons (45ml) wheat flour

3 cups (750ml) water

½ teaspoon (2ml) glycerine

1 teaspoon (5ml) dish detergent

Blend the flours together in a saucepan with a little water. Add the remaining water and cook over medium heat, stirring constantly, until the mixture resembles a thin custard. Remove the paste from the heat and stir in the glycerin and dish detergent to keep the paste smooth and pliable.

𝓒ORNSTARCH RECIPE

Mix ¼ cup (60ml) cornstarch with ¼ cup (60ml) water until well blended. Then add 1 cup (250ml) water and heat while stirring until the mixture resembles a thick custard. Finally, stir in ½ cup (125ml) water to thin it.

𝓒OLORING THE PASTE

Color can be added to either mixture immediately after cooking, by using a small brush to vigorously stir in 1 to 2 teaspoons (5–10ml) of watercolor, poster paints, or acrylic paints.

Use more or less paint depending upon the intensity of color desired, bearing in mind that the paste will dry a bit lighter than it looks in the container.

𝓟REPARING THE PAPER AND BRUSHING ON THE PASTE

Although you can often brush the paste on small (11- by 17-inch [27.5 x 42.5cm]) sheets of paper and make designs without first wetting the sheets, the paste sometimes dries out before you've completed a complicated design. Also, the paper will sometimes buckle up as you work it. Dampening the paper before applying the paste will keep the paste moist longer and allow more time to make the patterns. Some people simply dampen the sheet with a sponge and proceed, but we've found that the papers will often wrinkle from an uneven wetting and thus distort the patterns.

The best solution seems to be to place the sheet of paper in a sink or tray of water to evenly wet and relax it for a moment, and then hang it over a folding clothes rack or line for a minute to let it drip. Next place the sheet on a smooth, waterproof surface like a sheet of Plexiglas, and stroke it with a sponge to press out air bubbles and excess moisture. When the sheet is completely flat, you can apply the paste.

Dip a large 3-inch (7.5cm) paintbrush in your colored paste and brush it on as evenly as possible, covering the whole sheet with a thin layer of paste. You may want to brush horizontally at first and then go over the strokes from top to bottom to get a good color application. If you're using different-colored pastes on the same sheet, brush in only one direction to avoid mixing the colors. They'll blend slightly where they overlap, but the effect will be quite subtle and lovely.

■

PATTERN-MAKING PRINCIPLES

Allover repeat patterns sometimes referred to as diaper patterns are particularly effective designs in paste. A simple row of horizontal lines crossed by vertical ones at regular intervals can be quite eye-catching. Contrast in a paper can be achieved by varying the thickness of a line or by placing a wavy line next to a straight one. Circular motifs enclosed in square or triangular boxes also command attention.

As you begin making designs, many pattern-making principles will reveal themselves. You'll find that overlapping certain patterns gives a sense of

dimension. Varying the type of mark you make (hard-edged versus soft) is also effective. Simple stripes drawn over the soft blurred impression left by a hair pick or finger marks can be visually stimulating.

Many people begin with symmetrical designs and concentrate on creating straight lines intersecting in various places. Images like these are reflective of many historical designs. Eventually you'll want to create some asymmetrical papers, however, to explore the contemporary images and unique prints you can also make in paste.

■

PASTE-PAPER TECHNIQUES

*C*OMBED PAPERS

After you've applied your paste, begin a combed sheet by choosing a patterning tool and drawing it through the paste. As it pushes the paste aside, the tool reveals the paper color beneath it. If the paste begins to run back into the corridor you've created, it's too thin and should be thickened to prevent creating weak designs.

Use a firm but gentle approach as you work to prevent inscribing or tearing the damp paper. Vary the direction and type of movement to create straight lines or curves with the tools.

The papers located on page 40 show how various comb movements alter a design as they're done in succession over each other.

■ **OPPOSITE PAGE:** *Plastic hair picks and steel wood-graining combs were used to create these paste-paper designs. The texture and color of the Canson paper (the larger piece) add impact to the finished sheet.*

■ **FIGURE 4-1.** *Draw your patterning tool over the paste-covered sheet in a wavy or straight motion. Short choppy strokes are also effective.*

4-1

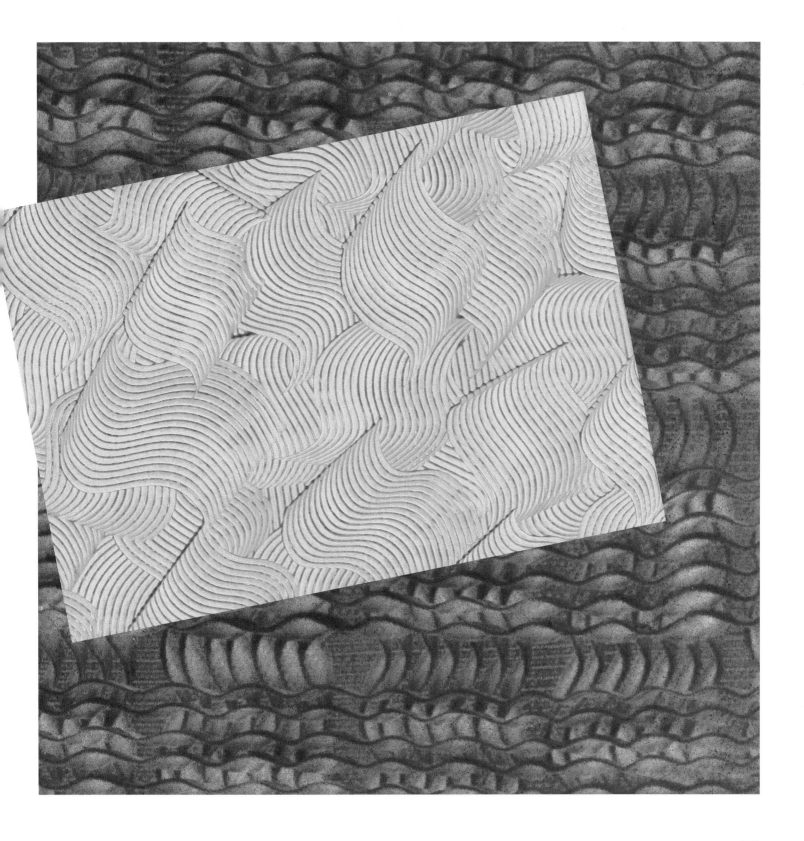

ℬRUSH IMPRESSIONS

One of the most important rules to understand if you're going to make art is that sometimes it's best to break all the rules. A deliberately haphazard paste application (contrary to the instructions for brushing on the paste) can yield beautiful sheets that need no further embellishment. Using brushes of various widths in a slapping motion with or without paste on them can create fascinating waved and featherlike images. The sound the brush makes as it strikes the paste is liberating as well. (It's the same sound your fork used to make in those forbidden mashed-potato sculptures we all created as children.)

𝒮PONGE IMPRESSIONS

Dabbing sponges of various shapes and sizes into the paste will leave mottled patterns in your paste papers. You can trim the sponges or enlarge the holes to accentuate the impressions they make. You can also apply additional colors with a sponge over a previously printed sheet to create interesting designs.

𝒫RINTS IN PASTE

Intricate allover patterns can be made on a brushed sheet by stamping into your paste with various objects. Pieces of dowels or squares of balsa wood can be cut to create geometric shapes. Various rubber, cork, metal, and wooden objects can be used to strike the pasted paper. A blurred impression will be left where the object displaces the paste.

Wooden rolling pins with carved designs and carved rubber printmaking brayers will leave good impressions if your paste is made a little thicker than usual. If your design is cut intaglio (causing a depression in the surface of the material), the cut areas will be printed, as the areas around them lift the paste away. If the design is raised from the surface of the brayer or other material (a relief image), the area surrounding the design will be left in the paste, as the relief image displaces the paste.

𝒫ULLED PAPERS

If two brushed papers are pressed together face-to-face and then pulled apart, amazing landscape-like formations will result.

Experiment with stiff and thin pastes to vary the images, which can range from intricate, feathery veined patterns to bold mountains and valleys. String and lace can be sandwiched between the sheets to enhance the designs, or different-colored pastes can be applied to parts of each sheet to later mix with the colored paste with which it makes contact.

𝒮PATTER PAPERS

You can push very thin colored paste through a sieve to cover a sheet with a fine spray of color. You can also dip a toothbrush into the paste and draw your thumb across the bristles to spray it on a sheet of paper. There's no need to dampen the paper if you apply the paste with these methods and don't intend to pattern them further.

𝒱ARYING THE TEXTURES

Use thick or thin paste to create different types of textural interest in your work. At one time you may be seeking a smooth, glossy finish on a paper to be used as a tiny book cover. At another time, a paper with a coarse, grainy texture might be sought after to use as a lampshade on a lamp with a pottery base. If you make a thick paste, the hills and valleys created by drawing through it will remain after the paste is dry.

I gave a paste-paper demonstration at a local art center last year and was happy to see a young blind woman show up with her sighted companion. She'd been at several of my marbling demonstrations but could only listen as I described the images I was creating. This time, because I was using a particularly thick flour paste mixture, she could actually feel the designs on the dry paste papers.

■

FINAL STEP: DRYING THE PAPERS

You can dry your decorative papers by draping them over a rack or line or laying them on sheets of newspaper. If you let them dry on the Plexiglas on which they were sponged down, they'll dry quite flat. You can also press them under books or boards or iron them.

■ **OPPOSITE PAGE:** *These papers show the patterning steps used to create the train schedule shown on page 107. First a sheet of paper was coated with paste and a wood-graining comb was used to make rows of vertical stripes, creating a background design (center). A multiple-line pen was used to make horizontal stripes spaced about 1 inch (2.5cm) apart over the first pattern to depict train rails (right, bottom section). The railroad ties were created by making short strokes in the paste with a plastic spackle knife (right, top section). Finally, a thin strip of cardboard was coated with paste and pressed between the rails to suggest grassy areas (left).* **RIGHT:** *A thick application of paste helped create this pulled paste-paper landscape.*

$\mathcal{D}$irect Printing

$\mathcal{D}$irect printing is one of the oldest and simplest means of creating a decorative repeat design. Used since the sixth century as a method of decorating fabric, direct printing is easily adapted to be used on paper.

Anything that can be inked and then pressed against paper can be used for this type of paper decoration. You can print with found objects to practice what some people call junk printing. You can also intricately carve and incise linoleum blocks for sophisticated images, or create raised printing surfaces by gluing various materials such as cardboard or rubber to wooden blocks.

Even common fruits and vegetables can be used as direct-printing stamps with success. Sometimes the printing vehicle is recognizable, but often an overlapping design, printed out of register and in a different color, looks so complicated that an onion or potato stamp is never suspected.

■ **OPPOSITE PAGE:** *This linoleum-block print by Laurie R. Wicker is a section of a 15½- by 25-inch (39 x 63cm) paper. Laurie used acrylic paints with metallic and iridescent flecks on Moriki paper.* **ABOVE:** *This collage of torn and dyed paper with rubber-stamp printing is actually the cover of a photo album. It measures 11 by 14 inches (28 x 35cm) and is the work of Gail Crosman-Moore.*

■

EQUIPMENT AND MATERIALS

You'll need various types of tools, depending upon the type of block or stamp you're creating, but the basic equipment includes the following:

- Cutting implements, such as X-Acto knives or craft knives, to inscribe or carve out most soft-surface blocks. For harder linoleum or wood blocks, you may want linoleum-cutting gouges (available at art-supply stores).
- A soft pencil will be needed for outlining areas of blocks to be carved.
- A piece of Plexiglas or an old cookie sheet can be used for spreading and mixing ink. This will become your inking tile.
- A roller or soft printmaking brayer from an art-supply store is useful for rolling ink directly onto a stamp or onto the inking tile from which it will be picked up.
- Foam polybrushes commonly sold in paint stores can be used in place of brayers to evenly pat ink onto many printing surfaces.
- A small watercolor brush will be helpful for blending inks and for applying inks to small printing surfaces.
- Sponges, helpful for cleanup, also make good simple stamp pads.
- Newspaper will be used to cover tabletops, to absorb excess inks from printing surfaces, and to create a padded printing surface on which to work.
- Surgical gloves or barrier hand cream.

Paper

Printing can be done on various types of paper. Soft printmaking papers such as those made by Bienfang, Aquabee, Strathmore, and Speedball are ideal. Hand-made papers and imported papers like Fabriano and Aquarelle can be used for special projects. Many drawing and painting papers, like the numerous types of charcoal, etching, and Oriental papers, will also serve you well. Use colored as well as white sheets to extend the range of your printing palette.

Color

Watercolor, tempera, and acrylic paints all yield good images. They can be thinned or used full strength, depending upon the consistency. Special block-printing inks can be purchased from an art-supply store in either water or oil bases. Although the oil-base inks sometimes have a richer color, they also have some pretty noxious fumes.

If you want to work in oils and don't mind the more extensive cleanup involved, there are many to choose from. Tube colors, silk-screen inks, and printers' inks all work fine. Be sure to follow safety precautions and work in a well-ventilated area or use a respirator, if possible.

■

PATTERNING PRINCIPLES

Many of the design principles observed in making paste papers will be useful to remember when making decorative printed papers. Contrast, rhythm, and movement will be determined by what kinds of images you place next to each other, how much distance exists between various shapes, and how strong an impression you make as you press your printing block against the paper.

It's important to realize that the negative space between the printed areas also forms a shape. This negative space will attract and hold your eye as much as the positive inked areas. Also, the weight and color of the inked impression will determine whether it recedes into the background of a design or becomes one of the focal points of a sheet.

Experiment by overlapping shapes to create new ones. You can print over a dry printed image, continue to stamp even though your inked surface is almost dry, and create diagonal as well as horizontal and vertical designs. Keep a notebook of what you feel are particularly effective ways of creating shapes, along with samples of successful papers, to give yourself a repertoire of designs to build on from session to session.

■

DIRECT-PRINTING TECHNIQUES

*V*EGETABLE AND FRUIT PRINTS

Vegetables such as potatoes, carrots, onions, and turnips can be cut in half or sectioned to be used as printing surfaces. Paint can be patted on the vegetable to ink it, or a sponge can be soaked with color to

become a makeshift stamp pad. You can repeat shapes in various ink colors, or incise the vegetables by carving out parts of the printing surface. Because vegetables are soft and easily cut, they can be easily sculpted into plant, animal, and geometrical shapes. More abstract images can be made by scratching into areas of the vegetable in order to give it a textured surface.

Citrus fruits can be used for printing with some success, as well. Blot out some of their juice before inking them. Keep in mind that watercolor paints seem to mix best with citrus stampers. Because of their high water content, they tend to resist and smear oil paints.

*P*RINTING WITH FOUND OBJECTS

Most relatively flat surfaces that are too large to be pressed against a makeshift stamp pad can be inked with a poly sponge or brayer and printed. To ink the brayer, squeeze out several inches of tube paint or several teaspoons of ink onto the inking tile. Roll the ink horizontally, vertically, and diagonally to spread it and evenly coat the brayer. Then roll the brayer over your object until the ink is evenly dispersed. Finally, stamp the paper to transfer the image.

Old tools, washers and gaskets, kitchen implements, old wooden type, alphabet blocks, wire mesh, radio parts, and even fish skeletons can be used as textured stamps. Hardware stores and flea markets can yield hundreds of printing devices to use individually in a repetitive design or to use in conjunction with other shapes.

■ *An old gear and square nut were rolled with acrylic paint and used to produce this junk print (**top**). A carved potato stamp was used to create this watercolor fish print (**middle**). Soft linoleum was carved and rolled with several printing inks to make this double-helix design (**bottom**).*

𝒫RINTING WITH CARVED AND INCISED BLOCKS

Various materials can be carved into relief designs to transform them into printing blocks. Shapes that were successful when carved into vegetable bases can be recut in a more permanent material for repeated use. Styrofoam, balsa wood, cork, and the new soft linoleum produced for novice printmakers can be easily carved or scratched to produce a textured surface. Usually an X-Acto knife with a #11 blade will do the trick.

Battleship linoleum and hard rubber printing block sold in art-supply stores will make more permanent printing tools. Inexpensive sets of carving gouges can be purchased to carve these heavier materials.

For simple designs, begin creating your printing surface by outlining a simple shape on the block and penciling in all the areas you want to print. Then simply carve away all the areas you don't wish to appear as part of the design. Detailed designs can be made by incising the block and removing parts of the interior areas of the design as well. Ink and print your design as you work to check your progress. These sample prints, or proofs, can assure you that you're removing the correct areas. If you're carving a letter form, remember that you'll be printing a mirror image of what you carve.

If you know that you'll want to use the block you're creating in a repeat pattern of even rows, you may want to make a small notch at the edge of your block. It will help position it and can be used as part of the printed design, too. You could also rule chalk guidelines to help line up images or print by eye, allowing for slight imperfections in the design.

Don't be concerned that you don't have exceptional drawing skills; a repeat pattern of very simple forms often has more impact than more elaborate ones. If you find your confidence hopelessly flagging when you sit down to carve the block, you can always trace a design onto it and use that as a starting point. Simply place a piece of carbon paper over your block and hold the design you wish to trace over that. Then use a pencil or pointed implement to trace over the design and transfer the ink to the block.

Inspiration for your own designs and sources for traceable ones can be found in many places. Wallpapers, wrapping papers, and books on decorative arts or surface design can give you ideas of what other people have done to create allover designs. There are also a number of books of copyright-free illustrations that can provide you with illustrative materials. Have a photocopy made of designs you intend to trace so you have an unbound sheet to work with, or trace them out of the books, as well as onto the printing blocks.

PRINTING WITH BUILT-UP BLOCKS

An assortment of found objects can be glued to a wooden base to form a printing block. Be sure to use a waterproof glue if you intend to clean and reuse the stamp. Waterproof glue can also be used to mount various thicknesses of string or strips of wood to create a printing block with an interesting linear design.

Pieces of cardboard or inner tubes can be cut with scissors and glued to a wooden base to form another type of relief image. You can tear, scratch, or punch

out parts of the cardboard to achieve different textural effects. Be sure to coat the cardboard with a waterproof sealer if you plan to reuse it.

PRINTING WITH ROLLERS

Printmaking brayers can be rolled onto an inked surface and then rolled onto paper to transfer a wash of color. A simple split-fountain image can be obtained by rolling one color next to another and letting them overlap to create new blends of color. The areas where the inked rollers begin to dry become parts of the design.

Because rollers are made of varying degrees of softness, it's fairly easy to find one you can incise or carve to create a rolling printing device. The principle is the same as that used in making rolled paste papers, except that in this case you're depositing color instead of removing it. Pieces of felt or rubber can also be glued to a brayer to create another type of raised-design rolling printer.

READY-MADE PRINTING BLOCKS

Carved woodblocks similar to those used during the Middle Ages to print books can still be found today. Antique stores often contain fabric printing blocks used in India during the last century. These can be inked with a roller and used to make decorative papers. Alternating a design of your own with a repeat of the ready-made block print can yield interesting papers.

PRINTING WITH RUBBER STAMPS

Most of us have printed with a rubber stamp at one time or another. Their increasing popularity has made them easy to find in recent years; there are several companies that specialize in creating stamps depicting everything from fireflies to cityscapes. Colored stamp pads abound. You can stamp in fluorescents and iridescents as well as in earthy colors. Most stationery and art-supply stores also sell embossing powders that will give a stamped image a raised metallic surface when heated.

Some paper decorators like to play with these stamps and combine images to create overall designs. For really unique stamps that have an original look, though, you'll want to start from scratch.

To carve your own rubber stamps, use the same techniques discussed for carving heavier materials, bearing in mind that because erasers are soft, it's easy to miscut and ruin them. Choose a firm eraser and work slowly and carefully. You'll need the following:

- Good hard, not squishy or crumbly erasers. We found that Eberhard Faber Pink Pearl and Staedtler Mars Plastic Grand erasers were easy to carve.
- Small carving tools such as X-Acto knives with various-sized blades (#11 is our favorite). Small linoleum block V-gouges are especially useful for removing nonprinting background areas.
- Tracing paper and carbon paper if tracing a design from another source.
- Soft pencils for drawing designs on the erasers.
- Various-colored ink pads used for stamping in the traditional manner or some sort of an inking slab, and rollers or brushes to color-coat your stamp for printing. Very small stamps can sometimes be coated by applying felt-tip markers to their surfaces. Metallic markers give the best results as they dry more slowly than others.

In designing your own rubber stamps, you'll be following in the footsteps of the pharaohs of ancient Egypt, whose incised signature seals were the forebears of our modern rubber stamps. You'll have an easier time of it, however, as rubber erasers are a good deal easier to carve than bone or stone (or linoleum block, for that matter).

■ *Cotton string glued to a block of wood was coated with acrylic paint and stamped on black paper to produce this linear decorative paper (top). An eraser was carved to create the cat stamp; the end of a wooden dowel was used to make the cat's ball (bottom).*

Orizomegami

There are several ways to decorate paper based on the Japanese art of folding and dyeing paper known as orizomegami. In the traditional Japanese fashion, absorbent rice papers are folded and dip-dyed in bowls of vegetable dyes. But brushes and squeeze bottles can also be used to apply dyes directly to various parts of the folded paper bundle. A kind of tie-dyeing, too, can be used to decorate paper. Uncolored areas will be preserved where bindings prevent the dye from being absorbed.

The images achieved with these methods vary, but you can count on producing interesting, if not extraordinary, patterned papers with any one of them. The intricate kaleidoscopic designs that emerge when the papers are unfolded are quite surprising. The most difficult part of this kind of paper decorating is, in fact, waiting for the papers to dry so you can unveil them!

■

EQUIPMENT AND MATERIALS

You probably already have most of the materials needed for paper dyeing on hand. The only exception may be absorbent rice paper, which is readily available from art-supply stores. Although their shape and size will limit your folding options, coffee filters can be substituted for rice paper to get you started. You'll also need the following:

- A plastic cloth to cover your work area. Newspapers will be placed on top of this, but sometimes the dyes soak through them.
- Newspapers to cover the plastic-draped work area and absorb dyes from the drying bundles of paper.
- A hand towel for blotting moistened papers.
- A large amount of paper towels to be used for blotting dyed bundles of paper.
- Shallow jars, cans, or wide-mouthed cups to hold dyes.
- Rubber gloves to protect your hands from the dyes.

Paper

Patterns made with dyes are most effective on absorbent rice papers. Block printing papers, hand-made papers, calligraphy papers, and various kinds of *washi*—Japanese papers—will give dramatic results. Harder Western papers can be used, but they don't absorb colors as rapidly or as completely. Unless you're looking for very subtle coloring, you may be disappointed. Still, it's worth trying various types of paper for different effects. Unfortunately, the paper

■ **OPPOSITE PAGE:** *This orizomegami paper was folded in horizontal, vertical, and diagonal directions and then dipped in Japanese dyes.*

towels and newsprint that look so terrific after you've used them for blotting aren't good candidates for orizomegami. They won't stand up to the necessary folding and soaking. Wrapping tissue is also too fragile for most wet fold-and-dye procedures.

Color

Various types of inks and dyes will give good results. Food colors, Rit dye or other cold-water dyes, and Japanese liquid pigment inks are ideal. Experiment.

■

TECHNIQUES

𝒫LEATING AND DYEING

You can fold or pleat your paper in many ways to prepare it for dyeing. The hill-and-valley folds, also known as accordion folds, are the basis for most designs. You've probably done accordion folding in grade school. Since it's probably been a while, here's the refresher course.

Begin by folding your paper in half lengthwise, or horizontally. Then continue to fold each section formed in half again. If you turn your paper and fold away from you each time, you'll soon master the process.

When you can no longer fold in that direction, take the pleated bundle of paper and fold it crosswise, into a smaller square or rectangular bundle of paper. You might also try folding it back upon itself to form triangular sections.

6-1

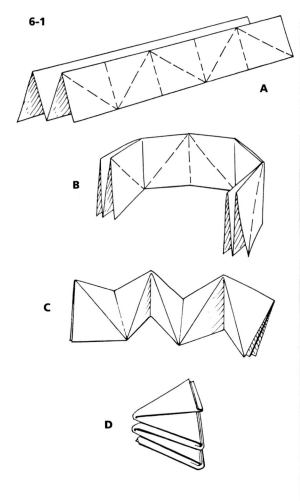

- FIGURE 6-1.

  A. *Fold a rectangular sheet of paper in half lengthwise, then fold each section in half again to form the hill and valley pleats shown.*

  B. *Fold the pleated bundle back on itself in the opposite direction. Turn the paper away from you each time you pleat to produce the desired accordion folds. You can brush-dye or dip-dye this square bundle of paper, or divide and refold each square section formed to make a triangular pleated bundle like the one shown in steps **C** and **D**.*

6-2

- *The finished papers from figure 6-1 (**top**) and figure 6-2 (**bottom**).*

- FIGURE 6-2.

  A. *Make narrow accordion pleats (about ¾ inch [1.9cm] wide) in a sheet of paper.*

  B. *Fold the pleated bundle in half, then fold each of these sections in half again to complete the folding pattern.*

6-3

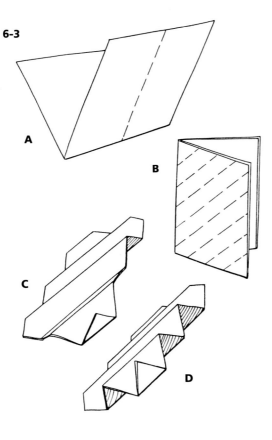

■ **FIGURE 6-3.**

A. *Fold the paper in half crosswise so that it's open at the top.*

B. *Fold it in half again.*

C. *Diagonally accordion-pleat the entire folded paper.*

D. *Bring all pleated sections together to brush- or dip-dye.*

■ *The finished papers from figure 6-3 (**bottom**) and figure 6-4 (**top**).*

■ **FIGURE 6-4.**

A. *Fold the paper in half lengthwise.*

B. *Starting from the center, fold the paper in narrow pleats to the left and then to the right until you've pleated the entire sheet.*

C. *(Side view) Bind the paper with clothespins, if necessary, to make it easier to dye.*

6-4

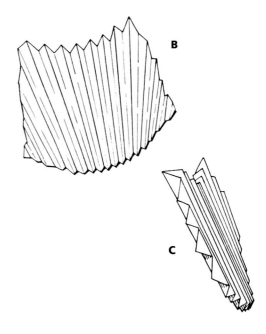

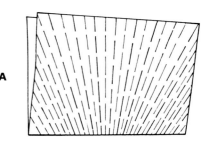

6-5

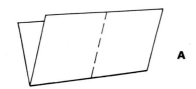

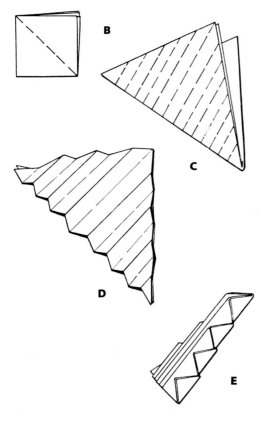

Moisten your folded paper bundle in water until it is evenly saturated. Carefully press out most of the water with your fingers and then blot it with a hand towel until it's just damp.

Next, pour some of your color into a shallow container and dip a corner of the damp bundle into the dye. The absorbent paper will act like a wick, drawing the color deep into its folds.

Remove the folded paper from the color and blot the dipped corner with a paper towel to distribute the color and prevent its bleeding further into the bundle than you wish. Now dip a second corner into another color (or a diluted version of the same color), and repeat the procedure.

When all the corners of your folded paper bundle have been dyed and blotted, place it on several thicknesses of newspaper and wait until it's almost completely dry before unfolding it. If your papers aren't too thin, and you work carefully, you can sometimes unfold wet papers. But it's risky; wet rice paper is very fragile.

Now try dipping just the edges of a folded paper bundle into dye to see how that changes the pattern. You can edge- or corner-dip dry papers, too, but the soft stained glass look is most pronounced with predampened paper.

APPLYING THE DYES WITH APPLICATORS

Brushes and squeeze bottles can be used to apply dyes for a variation of orizomegami. Food colors and other dyes can be used in their original dropper bottles, or dyes and inks can be poured into a

- **FIGURE 6-5.**
  A. *Start with square paper. Fold the paper in half lengthwise.*
  B. *Fold it in half again.*
  C. *Bring the bottom left corner up to meet the top right corner, creating a triangular fold.*
  D. *Accordion-pleat the triangular folded paper.*
  E. *A side view.*

- **BOTTOM LEFT:** *The finished paper from figure 6-5.* **OPPOSITE PAGE:** *A diagonally folded paper was bound with clothespins in several places and colored with Pientex dyes to produce this tie-dyed design (**left**). Rewetting and redyeing a decorated paper a second time produced this orizomegami piece (**right**).*

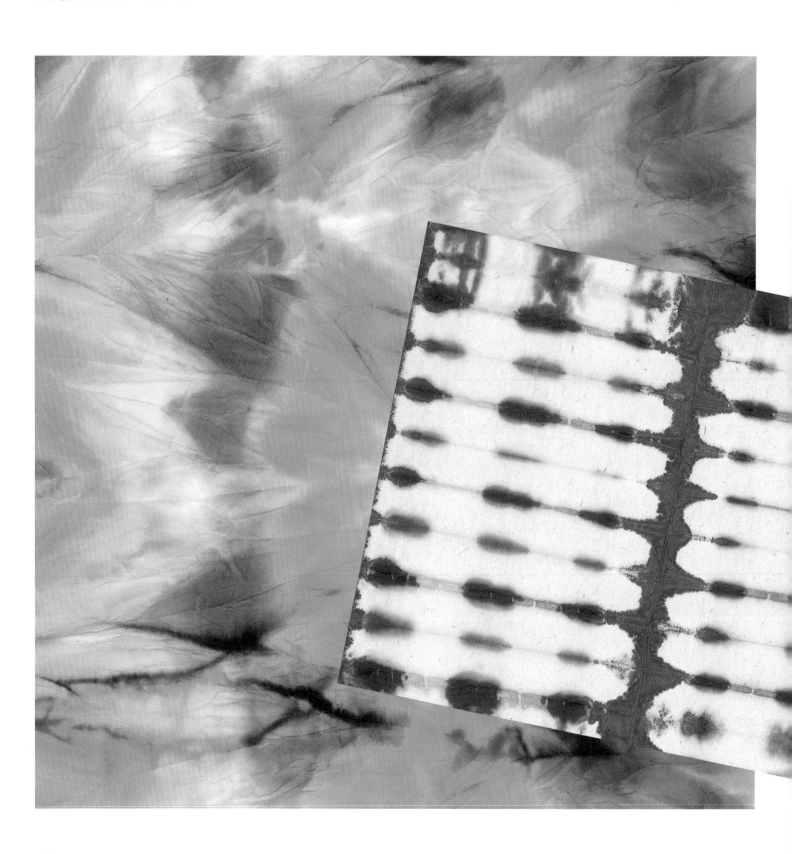

■ **OPPOSITE PAGE:** *These decorative papers were produced by crumpling and twisting a sheet before applying dyes with eyedroppers (**left**), and by binding a folded bundle with string before dip-dyeing (**right**).* **BELOW RIGHT:** *An ordinary coffee filter was ironed flat, folded over itself three times, and then brush-dyed to produce this kaleidoscopic image.*

container and applied with eyedroppers or small round paintbrushes. It seems easier to control the color bleed when applying the dyes with applicators than when dipping.

Try painting the color onto the front and back of a folded bundle for another type of image. This is most effective when there are just a few folds of thin paper so that a good dye penetration is possible. To distribute the colors well, be sure to blot the paper after the dyes have been applied.

You can further enhance a dye-decorated paper by refolding the sheet in a different configuration and redyeing it. Even adding a few more spots of dye to a dry, folded sheet can add interest to it. The red-and-orange patterns in one of my papers was pleasant enough, but not nearly as dramatic as when I redampened a spot and applied a few drops of food coloring to it. The wake marks, as well as the color, added much to the design. Sample folding patterns are located on pages 50 through 52. Try some of your own designs once you've mastered these.

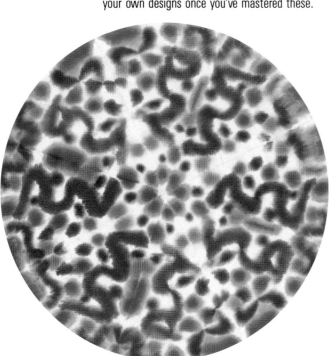

*T*IE-DYEING

Binding folded papers with string or clips before dyeing them will also alter patterns. The colors will pool in some areas and be prevented from reaching others. The resist areas will remain undyed and allow the color of the paper to show through.

Plastic clothespins are ideal for binding large folded papers and can be used as a handle for dip dyeing. They can be rinsed and used repeatedly. You can also bind with string or rubber bands, but be sure to leave the bindings in place until the bundle is dry to avoid tearing the paper when you remove them.

*C*RUMPLE AND TWIST DYEING

Instead of neatly folding papers to ready them for dyeing, you can bunch them into a ball or twist them. Some parts of the paper will receive dye, while others won't, lending a cloudlike, mottled appearance to the sheet. You can paint or dip-dye the bundle to color it. Try dyeing the bundle a second and third time to further color it, holding your papers in position by wrapping them with thread (if necessary).

■

FINAL STEP: FLATTENING THE PAPERS

Press your finished papers with a cool iron to flatten them. You won't be able to remove all of the creases, but the evidence of folding and bunching is meant to exist as part of the design.

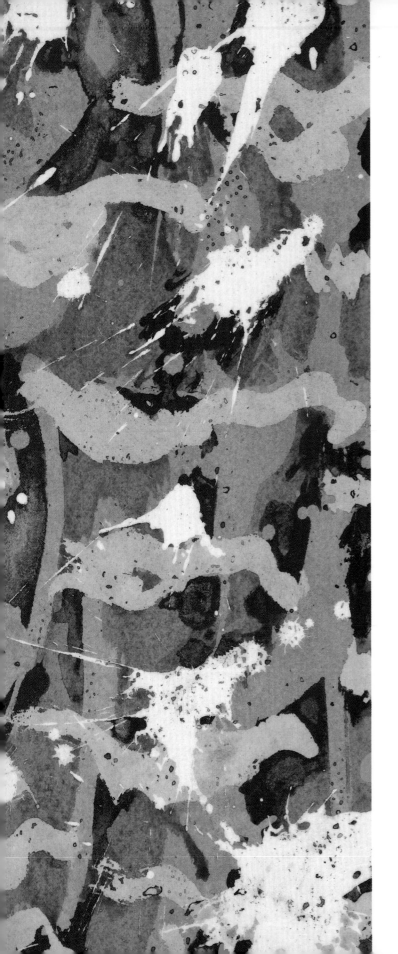

Batik

atik is a decorating technique, usually used on fabric, that flowered in Indonesia hundreds of years ago. Although it's still most commonly associated with fabric, batik is easily adapted for use with paper. The principle behind the process is simple: when wax is deposited on paper, it creates a waterproof barrier that prevents any colors that are applied from penetrating it.

If you use a piece of wax to draw a picture of a fish on a sheet of white paper, for example, and then coat the paper with a wash of red watercolor paint, you'll wind up with a red sheet of paper bearing the picture of a white fish, because the wax repelled the color in that area.

Various types of wax resists, from simple crayon resists to more complicated wax overlays, can be used to create stunning images. Multiple waxings and paintings can produce papers with a luminescence that resembles stained glass.

■ **OPPOSITE PAGE:** *"Flamingos" by Barb Webb. This watercolor batik, created by painting and splattering wax on a heavy watercolor paper, is 9 by 12 inches (23 x 30cm).* **RIGHT:** *This simple crayon batik was made by rubbing a crayon over a sheet of paper held against the metal head-board of an antique bed and then applying a watercolor wash over the design.*

EQUIPMENT AND MATERIALS

- A double boiler should be used to safely melt the wax.
- Cheap disposable watercolor brushes in small and large sizes should be used for applying wax. Wide watercolor brushes or polyfoam paintbrushes are used for applying the wash of color.
- An iron for removing the wax from papers.
- Lots of newspaper to protect tabletops and to absorb wax as it's ironed out of a print.
- Color containers for each color used.
- A #2 pencil can be used to lightly draw designs to be waxed, if desired.
- Optional: pipe cleaners to be used as a wax-stamping device.

Wax

Paraffin or batik wax can be used for this process. Candles and crayons can be used to draw resists on paper.

Paper

Many kinds of paper, including watercolor papers and even typing paper are fine for batik. Very thin or absorbent papers aren't recommended for this type of paper decorating.

Colors

Liquid, rather transparent colors, like food coloring, liquid dyes, or cheap watercolors, are appropriate for batik on paper.

CRAYON OR CANDLE RESIST

The most basic type of wax resist is made by drawing a design on paper with a crayon or a candle and applying color over it. You can also hold your paper against a textured surface such as cement or stucco as you wax an area to make a rubbing. Then apply a wash of color, and when it's dry, iron it between layers of newspaper. The crayon or candle color will remain in a melted state as part of the design.

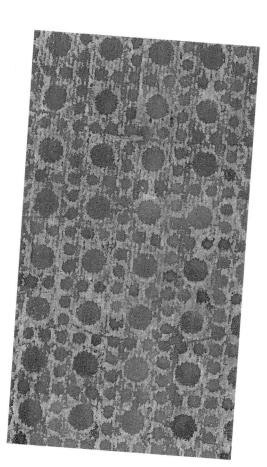

■

TRADITIONAL BATIK

Melt your paraffin in a double boiler, being careful not to overheat the wax, because this may cause it to give off noxious smoke and possibly start a fire. Then dip an inexpensive brush into the wax and make a number of waxed strokes on a white sheet of paper. You'll have to work quickly so that the wax doesn't dry in the brush before you've had a chance to deposit it on the paper. Make as many strokes as you like, bearing in mind that each of them will appear as white strokes in the final paper.

Next brush your first color over the entire sheet of paper. Start with a pale color, like yellow, for the first coat. Let the paper dry, and then brush on more wax. The designs made with this application of wax will be yellow, or the color you just dyed the paper. Apply another coat of color, and let it dry before adding another waxed design. Continue with as many coats of wax and color as you like, bearing in mind that each coat of wax will maintain the last color applied.

When the final coat of color has been applied and the paper has dried, sandwich it between several layers of newspaper and iron it. Keep changing the absorbent newspaper until all the wax has been melted out of the sheet.

You can be very methodical in your wax application, creating symmetrical repeat designs, or you can create free-form papers by splashing and splattering wax as you work.

In addition to applying wax with candles and brushes, you can also use a stamping device fashioned from a twisted pipe cleaner. Twist most of the cleaner into a flat design. Let a few inches (centimeters) extend straight up, though, so you'll have a handle to work with.

■ **BOTTOM LEFT:** *The dramatic effect of multiple waxings and colorings is shown in this abstract batik by Catherine Campbell. The work measures 8 by 10 inches (20 x 25cm).*
OPPOSITE PAGE: *The playful effects of brushing and dripping melted wax onto paper can be seen in these three designs.*

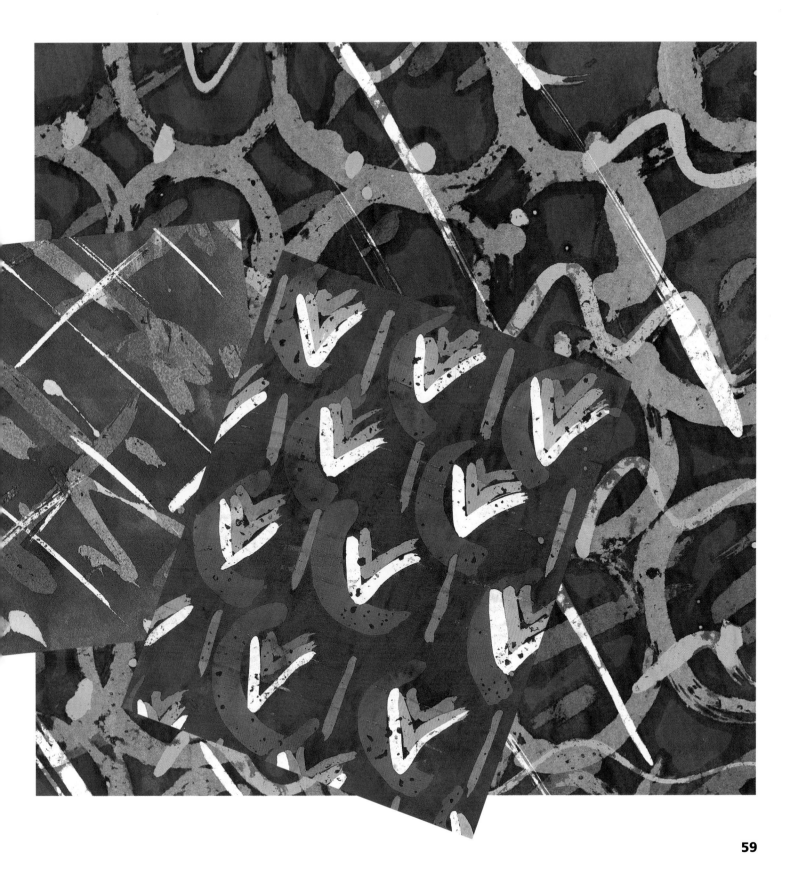

$\mathscr{S}$tencil Prints

$\mathscr{S}$tenciling, achieved by applying color through a decorative opening cut in heavy paper, was widely practiced in Europe during the fifteenth century as a means of decorating maps and playing cards. It was also popular during Victorian times, particularly in North America, as a method of depositing various motifs on furniture, walls, and ceilings.

Stenciling is now flourishing once again, as a decorative art used to produce romantic floral borders on ceilings, dazzling checkered patterns on floors, and a multitude of designs on lamps, books, boxes, and picture frames. Precut stencil designs and equipment to make stencils can be readily purchased in most fabric and department stores. You can adapt precut stencils, masking off parts of them or enlarging cut areas to modify them. When you see what an easy and direct method of paper decorating this is, however, you'll probably want to make your own.

8-1

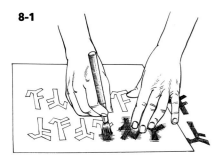

■ **FIGURE 8-1.** *Work on top of your stencil acetate and use circular dabbing motions to lay down a thin layer of color.*

■ **OPPOSITE PAGE:** *"Kilim Stencil," by Jennifer Philippoff. This 11- by 17-inch (28 x 43cm) stencil paper was made with acrylic paints.*
ABOVE: *"Poetry Quilt," by Joy Rodgers-Mernin, combines acrylic stenciling and calligraphy. The piece measures 28 inches (70cm) square.*

■

EQUIPMENT AND MATERIALS

- Acetate or stencil board can be purchased in most fabric and department stores. You can make a substitute by coating a manila folder with boiled linseed oil, but stencil acetate works better and is inexpensive. Since you'd probably have to go out to get the oil, you may as well get the acetate instead.
- An X-Acto knife with a #11 blade or a craft knife can be used for cutting the stencil. You can also fold the acetate in half and use scissors to cut out parts of it.
- A self-healing cutting mat, purchased from a fabric or art-supply store, is a good surface to cut on. Otherwise, cut on a piece of glass, but be sure to tape the edges so you won't nick yourself.
- A ballpoint pen or permanent marker can be used to draw designs on the stencil acetate. You could also use carbon paper to transfer designs from various picture sources.
- Removable cellophane tape can be used to hold stencils in place, if necessary.
- Stencil brushes and sponge daubers are usually used to apply color through the stencil. We tried applying color with a 3-inch (7.5cm) foam house-painting roller and found that it worked well. We use it to make most of our designs.

Paper

Any high-quality paper that's not too absorbent can be decorated with a stencil.

Colors

Acrylics, watercolor printing inks, and oil paint crayons are all good coloring agents. The paints should always be of a creamy, rather than runny, consistency.

■

STENCILING TECHNIQUES

After you've transferred a design to your stencil acetate and cut it out, place the stencil over the paper you want to decorate and tape it down. (You can try just holding it down the next time, but it is best to minimize problems at the start.) Now coat your color applicator with just a bare minimum of color; applying the paint sparingly will prevent it from getting under the stencil and blurring the edges of your design.

To apply color with a brush or dauber, hold the tool upright and then pat the area to be colored. Work on top of the acetate at first, moving in circular dabbing motions from the edge of the open area to its center, and laying down a thin layer of color. If you're depositing color with a roller, use it almost dry and exert just a bare minimum of pressure.

When you've finished printing, remove the tape and then the stencil by picking it straight up so that it does not slide and smudge the edges of your design. Wipe off any excess color from the stencil before moving it to a new position on your paper.

Now try cutting a stencil with several separate sections, depositing different colors in each of them.

$\mathscr{P}$aper cutting

$\mathscr{T}$he intricate cutting that goes into creating an elaborate stencil sometimes yields a design that deserves to be enjoyed for itself, rather than serving as a mask through which to apply paints. This became painfully self-evident to us one day, when the image we'd spent an hour creating from a detailed, multisectioned stencil was disappointing compared to the stencil itself.

But paper cutting is not just a poor relation to stenciling; it's a time-honored craft that dates back fifteen centuries in China. Paper cutting has a long and respected history in other parts of the world as well. The techniques have been passed from one generation to the next in Germany, Switzerland, and Poland. The detailed, fine cuttings that were done in Poland are especially amazing when you consider that many of them were made with a rather oversized cutting tool—sheep shears.

Roxanne Hutchison, a paper cutter whose meticulous work appears here, often works in the style of her Polish forebears to produce intricate designs. Although achieving a high level of skill takes years of practice, surprisingly detailed designs can be produced by a novice in just a few hours.

EQUIPMENT AND MATERIALS

Cutting simple designs requires only thin paper and a pair of sharp scissors (or sheep shears, if you like a challenge). For more intricate work, you'll probably want a #2 pencil for drawing designs, an X-Acto knife, and a cutting mat or taped sheet of glass on which to cut. Working on glass is preferable, as its smooth surface makes it easier to turn the paper as you work.

- **OPPOSITE PAGE:** *Detail of traditional paper cutting.* **RIGHT:** *"Coming Home" by Roxanne Hutchison. Handmade paper was used to create this intricate paper cutting. It measures 16 by 20 inches (40 x 50cm).*

- **FIGURES 9-1 to 9-4.** *To produce the paper cuts shown in the photograph on page 64, start with a square or rectangular sheet of paper and fold in the direction of the arrows.*

TECHNIQUES

Begin with a folded square of rice paper. You can fold the sheet in half if you want to make two identical designs. If you fold the sheet twice, each of the four sections formed will bear the design. Very intricate paper cuttings can be made by folding tissue-thin paper for as many as sixty-four repeats. Try some simple designs, with smooth flowing lines or sharp geometric cuts at first. Work deliberately, with as little hesitation as possible, and try to keep your cutting hand stable and turn the paper as you work. Make sure, too, that you have a fresh blade in your X-Acto knife if you are attempting to remove interior parts of a design.

Some folding designs, along with suggestions for cutting patterns, are located below and on page 64. Try your own free-form or penciled-in designs, too, remembering to always leave part of the folded edge intact so that all pieces of the design remain joined.

Paper cuttings can be strung, paper-doll style, between doorways to announce a celebration or mounted on backing papers with glue sticks or spray adhesive. Because they're so fragile, unless you have a particular use in mind, you may want to place the paper cuttings in a plastic sleeve to await their use in a paper project.

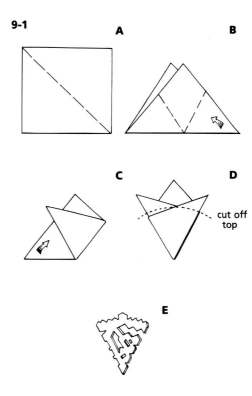

63

9-2

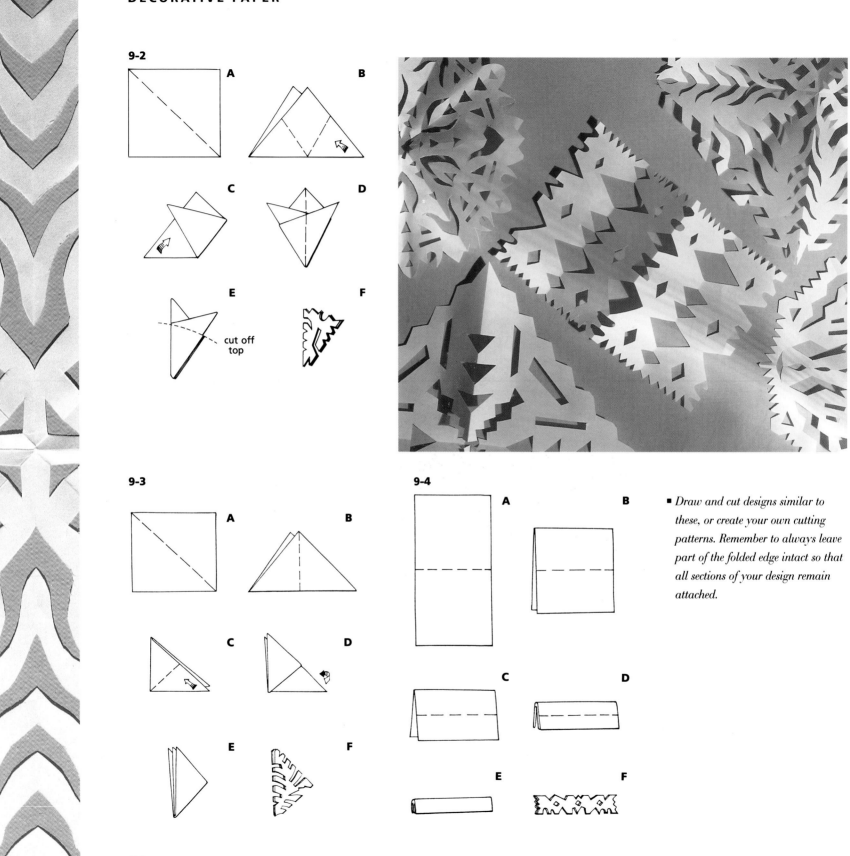

A

B

C

D

E

cut off
top

F

9-3

A

B

C

D

E

F

9-4

A

B

■ *Draw and cut designs similar to these, or create your own cutting patterns. Remember to always leave part of the folded edge intact so that all sections of your design remain attached.*

C

D

E

F

CONTEMPORARY PAPER SLITTING

An ordinary white sheet of paper can take on an architectural dimension if you alter it with a few simple slits and folds. It's not necessary to add anything to or remove anything from the sheet to decorate it. The subtle play of light and shadow on the cut and folded areas is often enough adornment to prove satisfying by itself.

*E*QUIPMENT

A cutting mat, X-Acto knife, and ruler will be needed for simple slitting experiments. If you want to play a bit more, you'll appreciate having a T square or triangle handy, so you can accurately line up repeat designs. You might also try laying out slitting patterns on a sheet of graph paper and cutting through it to accurately position your openings.

■ *An X-Acto knife and a metal ruler were used to transform Canson Mi Teintes and Strathmore cover stock into these contemporary note cards.*

*T*ECHNIQUE

One of the easiest ways to open a sheet of paper is to cut a number of small X shapes in it, and then fold the resulting paper flaps back. The Xs can be evenly spaced or appear randomly throughout the sheet. The design will be altered by the size of the slits created and the degree to which you open the flaps. You might choose to work in plain white paper, letting the openings and paper texture make your statement, or you could place a colored sheet (or another decorated paper) behind the openings. You could work with a two-sided paper or laminate two different-colored papers together before you begin slitting so that when the flaps of the X are turned back, a second color is revealed.

V-shaped, or horizontal and vertical openings resembling the parentheses and bracket marks of punctuation could be used to decorate a sheet. The templates used by graphic artists and engineers are especially fun to use; these are heavy plastic guides, rather like stencils, that have openings shaped like triangles, concentric curves, ellipses, etc., which you can trace or cut through.

Below are a few examples of slitting designs that you can try. We cut them in heavy cardstock to make a series of unique note cards.

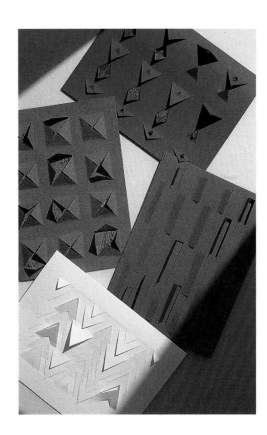

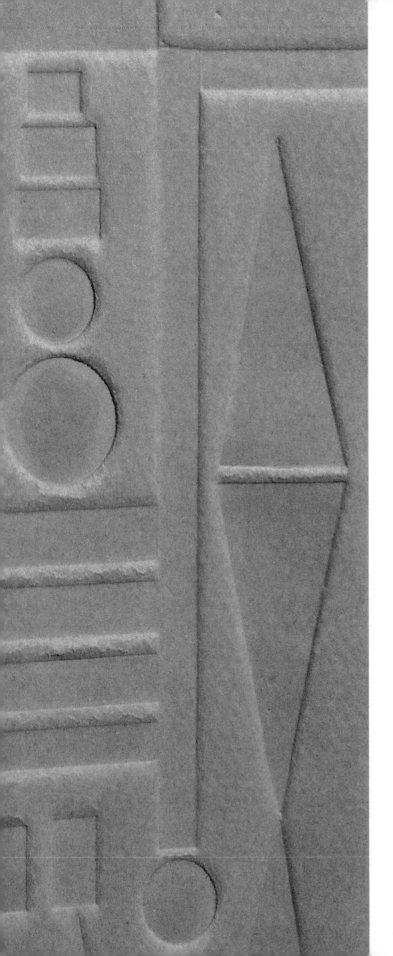

*E*mbossing

A raised or recessed design can be made on paper by embossing it. The monochromatic designs often seen on expensive stationery, and shown here in the work of Edie Roberts and Rose Brein Finkel, have a simple elegance. You can create similar decorative designs on your own papers and cards with little effort.

If you've just cut a stencil for a project in the stenciling chapter, you can probably trace its shape onto a piece of bristol board, cut it out, and use it to make an embossed design.

■

EQUIPMENT AND MATERIALS

- An X-Acto knife with several #11 blades or a swivel knife will be a good cutting tool.
- A self-healing cutting mat would be helpful. Or you can use a piece of glass with taped edges.
- Removable tape will help stabilize the paper to be embossed.
- Two-ply, plate-finish bristol board or lightweight mat board can be used to make the embossing pattern.
- Additional scrap bristol or mat board can be used as a base to mount the embossing pattern.

- Sobo glue or a glue stick can be used to attach the two above-mentioned boards.
- A burnishing tool, which is used to press the paper against the edges of your embossing pattern, will also be needed. A bone folder or ball-tipped burnisher would be ideal, but there are lots of things you can use as substitutes, such as the back and tail of a plastic comb, a tongue depressor, or smooth cuticle sticks.

Paper

Paper for embossing should be of a good quality, but not too heavy. Art papers like Canson, Strathmore, Rives, and other 100 percent rag papers will give you a good image. Handmade papers can also be used.

■ **OPPOSITE PAGE:** *Detail from "Geometric," a hand-embossed card by Rose Brein Finkel. The embossing plate was made from layers of mat board.* **BELOW:** *"Angel Fish" by Rose Brein Finkel measures 9½ by 7 inches (24 x 18cm). It was embossed on handmade paper from a design carved in linoleum. The colorful scales are made of Japanese rice paper.*

■

TECHNIQUES

Trace or draw a design in the center of a small sheet of two-ply bristol board, then carefully cut it out. Work slowly so the edges of your cutout will be smooth, not ragged.

When you're finished, you'll wind up with two patterns: one bearing a positive image, the other a negative one. If you're cutting out a star, for example, you'll wind up with a small piece of bristol board shaped like a star (the positive image) and another, larger piece of board with a star-shaped hole in it (the negative image). Both patterns can be used to make embossings.

To make a positive raised design, use a spot of glue to affix the star to a larger sheet of board. Then place your embossing paper over the star, tape it in place, and depress the paper around it with your finger, following the outline of your design.

Having a light behind your design will help you define the areas that need burnishing. Work over a light table if you have one or hold your design against a sunny window.

Now take the burnishing tool and move it around the edge of the hidden star until its clean outline appears. Go slowly; if you apply too much pressure you may tear the paper. Turn the board as you work to make it easier to follow the outline of the design. When you're sure you've burnished every section of the paper, untape the finished raised design.

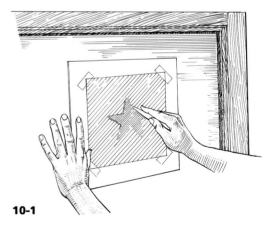

10-1

Now try using the negative design (the board from which the star was cut) to create a depressed design. Again, take your time as you work.

Some papers get quite shiny when they're burnished. If you like to make raised designs and don't want your paper to have a sheen, place a piece of tracing paper between your embossing paper and the burnishing tool.

$\mathcal{W}$ET EMBOSSING

Heavy papers that are difficult to emboss with dry embossing methods can often be made to cooperate by working with them in a dampened state. Although they're more fragile to work with, these papers often yield a crisper image. Be sure to coat your pattern with a waterproof sealer such as acrylic varnish if you plan to reuse it.

You can also emboss papers with various textured materials for allover designs. Damp papers can be pressed with scattered beans, rice, toothpicks, string, or found objects with a shallow relief design. At first, the papers will stretch around the objects they cover. When they dry, however, they'll shrink back and capture the image of the materials beneath them. It's much like embossing newly formed handmade papers, except that the papers can be dampened with a plant mister or sponge; they don't need to be soaked.

You can use a paper press, or simply some weighted boards, for this type of embossing. Begin this process by broadcasting your rice or embossing materials over the surface of a waterproofed board. Dampen the sheet to be embossed and place it over the rice. Then place a piece of blanket or a towel over the paper, and another board on top of that. Weight the stack with heavy books or jugs of water and leave the papers in place until they dry.

■ **FIGURE 10-1.** *Holding your design against a sunny window will help you define the areas to be burnished.*

■ **ABOVE:** *"Watermelon" by Rose Brein Finkel. Wetting the paper before embossing it helped define the water-melon seeds in this card.* **RIGHT:** *These embossings by Edie Roberts show how overlapping designs (**top**), using simple stencils (**center**), and burnishing over string or twine (**bottom**) can yield crisp results.*

Suminagashi

Suminagashi, the oldest form of marbling, is the ancient art of floating colors on liquid, patterning them, and capturing them by making a contact print. Suminagashi is also the simplest form of marbling, often overlooked by those involved with the more difficult varieties of the craft. But the subtle floating images, with their flowing veins of color, are gaining in popularity. And with good reason: pale images are the perfect background for letter writing and various forms of paper decorating. In a lamp shade or folding screen, the backlit rings and swirls of color have a luminescence that's unparalleled.

11-1

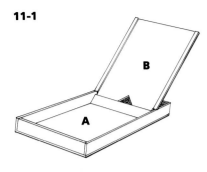

■ **FIGURE 11-1.** *The marbling tray with rinse board in place.*

■ **OPPOSITE PAGE:** *Marbling a sheet of paper, letting it dry, and then remarbling it produced this multiple-image suminagashi paper. The original, by Diane Maurer-Mathison, is 11 by 17 inches (28 x 43cm).*

■ **FIGURE 11-2.** *The material used to make the pieces in figure 11-1 should be lightweight and rigid, such as ½-inch (1cm) exterior plywood. The following instructions are for building a 20- by 30-inch (50 x 75cm) tray. You can use even thinner board if you are building a much smaller tray.*

1. Cut the following:

A. *1 piece 20" × 30" (50 × 75cm) for the base.*

B. *1 piece 20" × 30" (50 × 75cm) for the cover and rinse board, cut as shown.*

C. *2 pieces 2" × 30" (5 × 75cm) for the long sides.*

D. *2 pieces 2" × 19" (5 × 48cm) for the short sides.*

(continued on following page)

■

EQUIPMENT AND MATERIALS

Trays

In suminagashi, inks are floated on the surface of water. So the first piece of equipment you'll need is something to serve as a marbling tray to hold the water. A photo tray, large baking pan, or similar container about 2 inches (5cm) deep and large enough to accommodate the paper you wish to decorate will work fine, and you can fill the tray with plain tap water. You may eventually want to buy or build a professional tray with an attached rinse board. Directions for constructing a marbling tray appear below.

11-2

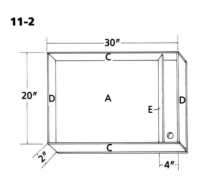

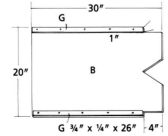

Shallow watercolor mixing trays will be ideal for holding your inks and dyes. You'll use only about a teaspoonful (5ml) of color at a time, so you won't need large containers. A small muffin pan can be used as a substitute color container. You will also need the following:

• Eyedroppers for depositing color in the small divided sections of the mixing tray.
• Gloves or barrier hand cream to protect your hands.
• Newspapers to help keep your worktable and drying area clean and to skim away dust and color that remains after each print is made.
• Clothesline or clothes drying racks hold wet papers.
• Optional: depending upon what types of colors and paper you use, you may want to use a large cookie sheet or other waterproof support for carrying papers to the sink or hose if they need rinsing. (Papers will need rinsing only if they fail to absorb all the ink and show color streaking.)

Brushes

Brushes will be needed to apply the inks. Inexpensive bamboo watercolor brushes in a #2 or #4 size are perfect. They're an inch (2.5cm) long and tapered. You'll want at least four of them.

Paper

Absorbent papers, like those used for orizomegami, are best for suminagashi. A few names to look for at your local art-supply store are Speedball block printing paper, and kozo, Moriki, and Okawara Japanese papers. Coffee filters and some handmade papers are also good to try. Some nonabsorbent papers, like typing paper, will pick up a marbled image, but the design will be pale and diffused.

Color

Kodak Photo Flo 200, a common darkroom supply, controls color floating and spreading in suminagashi. Some colors, like drawing inks, will float and spread without it, but most colors will benefit from 1 drop of Photo-Flo to about 1 teaspoon (5ml) of color.

A solution made by mixing 1 or 2 drops of Photo-Flo with 1 teaspoon (5ml) of water acts as a kind of invisible color. It will push out each circle of color it touches into a large narrow ring of color and preserve open areas in your designs.

Some colors used for orizomegami can be used for sumi marbling. Cake and liquid sumi inks, such as Boku Undo colors, work well. Drawing inks, such as Pelikan and Speedball inks, can also be used. The pigmented varieties work best. Even food coloring will give you reasonable results, although the image will be rather pale and soft edged.

■

TECHNIQUES

*S*KIMMING

Before you begin marbling and after you make each print, you'll want to remove the dust and excess color from the surface of the water. Some people believe that the easiest way to do this is to just lay a sheet of newspaper down on the water. When you pick it up, you'll remove unwanted debris. This method, however, will give you brand-new debris: a huge, sloppy, wet sheet of newspaper to dispose of. It's less wasteful and messy to cut 2-inch (5cm) wide

11-3

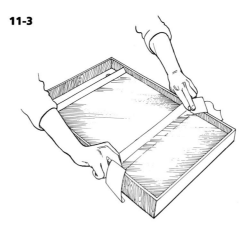

strips of newspaper and use them to skim off excess color. Hold the strip as shown and drag it over the water's surface. Skimming is especially important if you're using drawing inks; their residue will often prevent other colors from floating. If things get too dirty, of course, you can always change the water in your tray.

*T*ESTING THE COLOR

To see if your color needs Photo-Flo to make it disperse properly, transfer about 1 teaspoon (5ml) of color into your container and then dip your brush into the color. Wipe off any excess color, and then touch the tip of the brush to the surface of the water in your tray. The color should disperse quickly and spread to about a 3-inch (7.5cm) circle. If the color sinks or doesn't disperse enough, add Photo-Flo a drop at a time, stir it into the color well, and test again.

It's important to contain your enthusiasm and go slowly. Ironically, adding too much Photo-Flo will make your color sink. (It gets mixed with the water and alters the surface tension so much that colors can't push against it to float.)

(continued from previous page)

    E. *1 piece 2" × 19" (5 × 47.5cm) with one long edge cut at a 45-degree angle for the drain partition.*

    F. *1 piece 2" × 19" (5 × 47.5cm) for the skim board.*

    G. *2 pieces ¾" × ¼" × 26" (1.9 × .6 × 65cm) for the edge strips of the drain board.*

2. *Drill a ¾" (1.9cm) drain hole in one corner of the base.*

3. *Fill gaps in the wood with a wood filler, and sand smooth.*

4. *Glue together the edges of the tray and drain board, and clamp to dry.*

5. *Reinforce the tray corners, the bottom, the edges of the drain partition, and the rinse board strips with screws.*

6. *Sand the finished pieces and apply three coats of urethane or waterproof varnish.*

7. *Insert a 2" (5cm) piece of rubber tubing in the drain hole to help control splashing.*

■ **FIGURE 11-3.** *To skim, hold a newspaper strip as shown, making sure the ends of the strip drag against the sides of the tray. Pull the strip toward you, down the entire length of the tray. Bring it up and into the drain area of your tray to deposit the unwanted color residue.*

APPLYING AND PATTERNING COLORS

11-5

You'll use several brushes for suminagashi marbling: one for each color and one for the dispersant. Start with two brushes; load one with stirred, adjusted color and the other with the invisible color mixture (Photo-Flo and water). Barely touch the center of a water-filled tray with the color brush, releasing a drop of ink. Then touch the center of the circle of color that the ink has formed with the tip of the dispersant brush. It will propel the circle of color into a large ring.

If you apply your colors gently, you shouldn't have much sinkage. And if you're careful not to dunk the brushes underwater, you won't run the risk of diluting your colors.

MAKING A PRINT

You'll need to slowly lay a sheet of absorbent paper on the floating colors to make a print. If you shift the paper or flop it down as you apply it, you'll disturb the image and ruin the design.

11-4 A

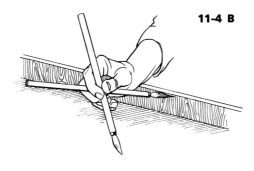

11-4 B

Alternately apply color and dispersant until a number of concentric rings are formed. Then gently blow them into a design. You could also fan the air above the marbling tray to coax the inks into a pattern.

Suminagashi masters traditionally held two color brushes in one hand and a dispersant brush containing a pine oil in the other. They usually worked in just two colors, black and indigo, and deposited between fifty and one hundred rings of color before patterning them. Use as many or as few colors as you like to create subtle or vivid designs.

11-6

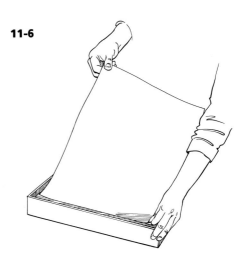

■ **FIGURE 11-4.**
   A. *Hold a color brush in one hand and a dispersant brush in the other to begin creating the suminagashi rings.*
   B. *After you're comfortable with that technique, try holding two color brushes in one hand and a dispersant brush in the other. It feels awkward at first, but it is easy to master and will help you deposit color more quickly.*

■ **FIGURE 11-5.** *You can fan or gently blow the floating rings into a design. You can also deliver a hearty burst of air from overhead to produce an image with jagged lines. Drag a single hair through the rings of color to produce yet another type of image.*

■ **FIGURE 11-6.** *Steady one hand at the far corner of your marbling tray and slowly roll the paper onto the floating color to make your suminagashi print.*

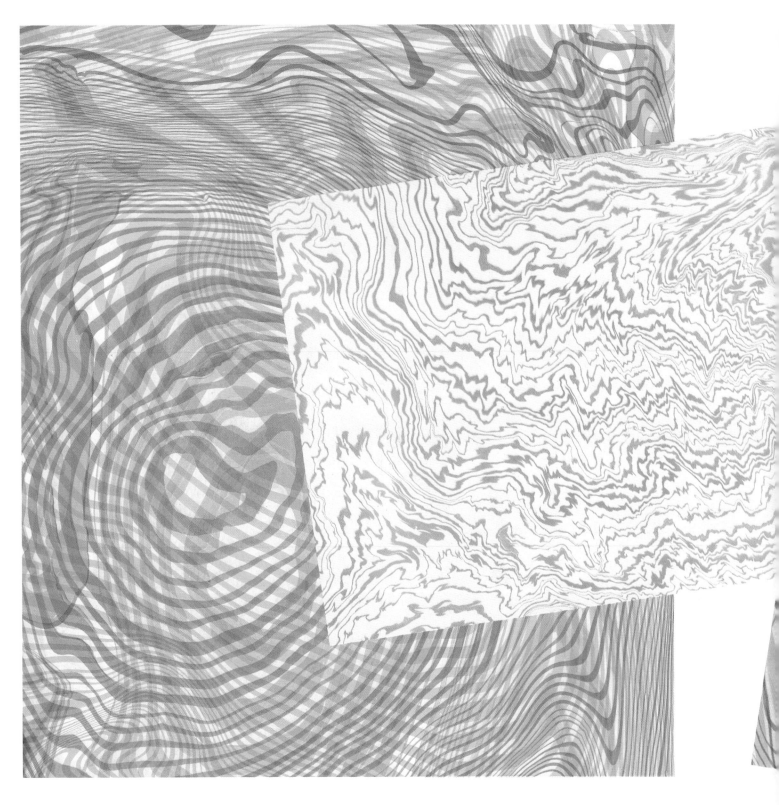

74

▪ *The single-image suminagashi paper at left center shows the jagged lines characteristic of prints made by blowing forcefully from above the floating rings of color. The intersecting lines on the other three multiple-image prints are the result of repeatedly marbling each sheet. The suminagashi dyes were patterned by gently blowing from the side of the marbling tray.*

An easy way to apply the paper is to hold it by diagonal corners so it droops in the middle; steady one hand on the far corner of the tray, and continuing to hold the paper, ease one edge onto the color. Then in one fluid motion, lower the rest of the sheet onto the floating colors. If you're working with very thin papers, you'll want to allow one edge of the sheet to remain dry so you can pick it up without tearing it.

When the sheet has made contact with the color, you can slowly peel back the paper and carry it to the drying area, or place it on a waterproof support for rinsing.

Altering the Image

Because the floating rings of color respond to the slightest movement, you can easily alter sumi images. You can blow gently from the side of the tray to create meandering lines of color, blow through a piece of tubing to pattern parts of the design, or deliver a hearty burst of air from overhead to create a pattern of jagged lines. You could also just let the natural movement of the spreading rings pattern the colors.

If you deposit rings of color in various sections of your tray instead of just working in the center of it, you'll also see a change in your patterns. But I think that the most exciting results are obtained by printing a second image on a dry printed sheet. The intersecting lines will create new patterns and colors. (Unfortunately the shellac-based drawing inks repel a second coat.)

Final Step: Flattening the Sheets

Most papers will lie quite flat if you press them under some large books. You can also iron them on a low setting.

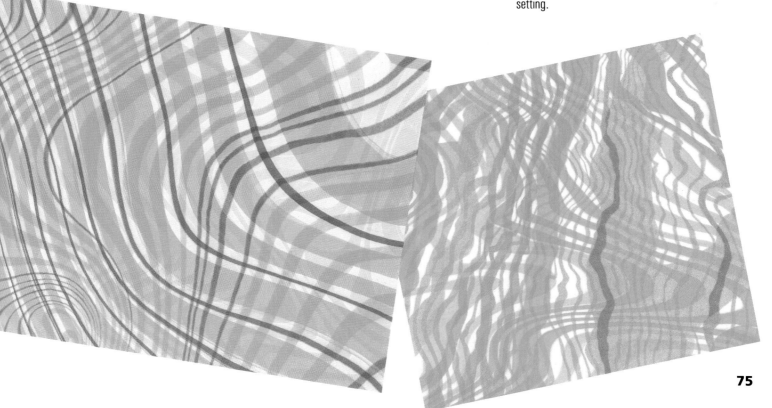

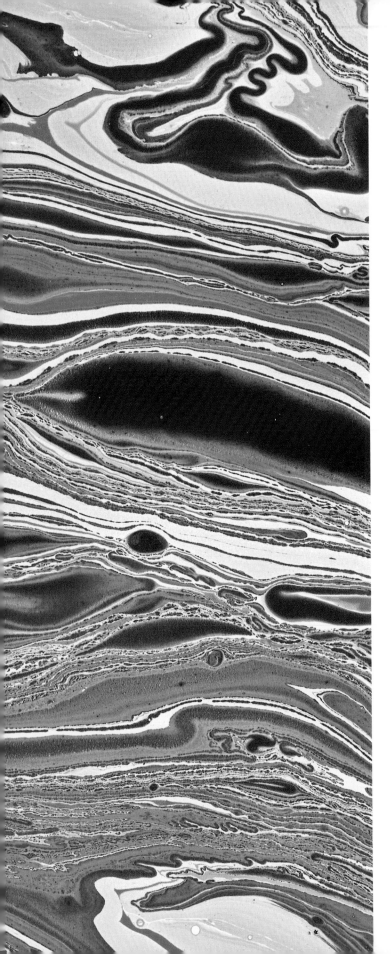

Oil Color Marbling

*O*il color marbling, like suminagashi, involves floating paints on a liquid, swirling them into patterns, and applying paper to make a contact print. Oil marbling has been practiced for centuries and was used extensively by European bookbinders as a means of decorating the endpapers and sometimes the covers of the books they made. Most large libraries have at least a few examples of eighteenth- or nineteenth-century books wrapped in paper with rich flowing swirls and spots of color—the distinctive mark of oil marbling.

There are two main types of oil marbling: one practiced by floating colors on water, another by floating colors on a marbling size. The size is a thick fluid made by adding various substances, such as methyl cellulose or powdered carrageenan, to water. The rapidly moving colors tend to loosely pattern themselves with the first method, but they can be combed to produce a more defined image on a marbling size. Either method will yield striking decorated papers with little effort and experience.

EQUIPMENT AND MATERIALS

Oil marbling will provide immediate gratification and yield uniquely patterned papers. There is a trade-off, however, because it's a rather messy and odorous process. Make sure your work space is well draped with plastic drop cloths and newspaper. Also be sure that you've got good ventilation (an exhaust fan, if possible) to protect yourself from oil-paint and thinner fumes.

Other equipment for marbling should include the following:

- A marbling tray. You can build one, purchase one, or use a substitute like the one suggested for suminagashi (see page 71). It cannot be the same tray, however, because the residue of oil paints left on tools and equipment would cause your sumi paints to sink.
- Newspaper skim strips and a receptacle for used ones.
- Extra newspapers and drying lines or racks.
- Glass or metal paint containers. Tuna or soup cans work fine.
- Color stirring sticks, such as dowels or Popsicle sticks.
- A mask to protect you from paint and thinner fumes.
- Protective gloves.
- Paper towels.
- Eyedroppers, small brushes like those used in suminagashi marbling, and broom-straw whisks for

depositing color. Whisks are indispensable for oil marbling. To make one, purchase a household broom and cut 6-inch (15cm) lengths of straw from it. Gather enough to form a 1-inch (2.5cm) bundle and bind it with a rubber band. You can use either the grassy or the stiff ends to deposit color.
- Water (plain tap water is fine).

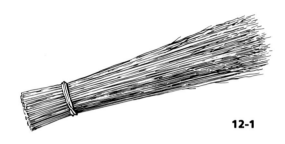

12-1

Paper

If a paper will withstand wetting and isn't so slick that it will repel paint, it can be used for oil marbling.

Colors

Oil colors can be purchased in either paste or liquid form. Paste colors include artists' oils, lithography and etching inks, and commercial printing inks. Liquid colors include Dryad Linmarblin colors, some house paints, and sign-painting colors. The gold-and-silver decorators' enamels, sold in hardware stores, are especially fun to use.

Use a drop or two of Photo-Flo to help problem colors spread. Linseed oil will brighten all colors and help soften paste colors. Mineral spirits are used to dilute oil colors, to help disperse color, and to clean equipment.

- **OPPOSITE PAGE:** *Oil marbling on water, by Sandra Holzman. The original measures 19 by 25 inches (48 x 63cm).*

- **FIGURE 12-1.** *Natural broom straw whisks, excellent for applying marbling color, are easy to make. Just gather a bundle of broom straw, cut it to a convenient size, and bind it with a rubberband. You'll need a separate whisk for each color used.*

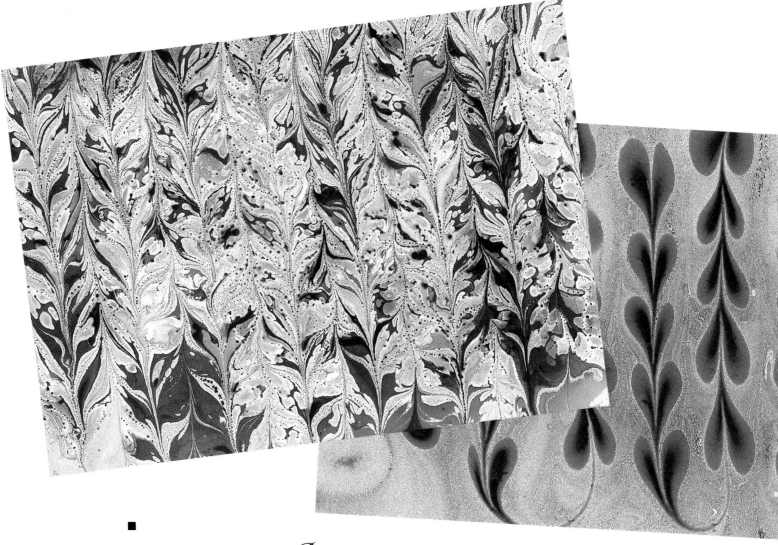

MIXING AND TESTING THE COLORS

*L*IQUID OILS

Pour about 1 inch (2.5cm) of well-stirred color into a container, add about one fifth as much linseed oil, and then add enough thinner to bring the color to a milky consistency.

*P*ASTE OILS

Start with about 2 tablespoons (25ml) paste color, and add about one fourth as much linseed oil. Using a large dowel or stick, push and stir the oil into the color until the paste becomes smooth. Now add a little more linseed oil (enough to bring the paint to a creamy consistency). When the color is well creamed, stir in enough thinner to bring the paint to a milky consistency.

Note: If the color is too stringy, you may have to use a mortar and pestle.

■ *When oil colors are applied to a marbling size, they can be patterned to a limited degree. These papers by Paul Maurer show the results of drawing a rake through whisk-applied color (**left**) and a stylus through color that was applied with an eyedropper (**right**).*

When your colors are thoroughly mixed, it's time to test them. To accomplish this, insert a whisk into the color, stir, and tap the whisk against the edge of the color container to remove excess paint. Then, holding the whisk above the water-filled tray, tap it against a dowel or your gloved forefinger to release some droplets of paint. If all is well, the paint will float and spread, but still retain its color.

12-2

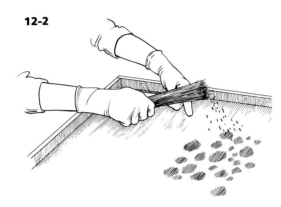

If the color spreads too much and becomes transparent, you'll need to add more paint to your mixture. If it sinks to the bottom of the tray, it's probably too thick and needs further thinning. When one color tests out okay, try another to adjust it for marbling.

Usually the colors will work together just fine. Sometimes, however, a particular color will alter the surface tension of the water in the tray so much that when the next color is applied, it can't spread enough to float. There are two ways out of this predicament: you can apply the colors in various sequences until you see which colors follow each other successfully, or you can add more thinner or Photo Flo to help the colors spread. Photo Flo may also cause some reticulation or novelty effects in certain oil paints—a bonus to its other properties.

■ **FIGURE 12-2.** *For an allover, random application of color, apply dye with a broom-straw whisk.*

■ **FIGURE 12-3.** *Use an eyedropper to methodically apply oil paints. When used on a marbling size, this type of color application can produce fantasy images like the one shown on the right of page 78.*

■

OIL-AND-WATER MARBLING

You can apply the paint with whisks and brushes or use eyedroppers to deposit paint in various sections of the tray. To use an eyedropper correctly, fill it with paint and keep pressure on the bulb as you move it to various parts of the marbling tray. You don't want to release the pressure and draw in air as you work or you'll deposit air bubbles along with paint. As soon as the paints touch the water, they'll begin to wander in and around each other to form their own designs. Apply as many colors as you like, using the color wheel on page 35 as a mixing guide.

Print by lowering a sheet of paper onto the floating colors, as outlined in the suminagashi chapter (see page 73). Work slowly so as not to trap air under your paper, which would cause a blank spot in your design. If you suspect that you have an air bubble in a sheet you've just laid down, tap it with your finger. Sometimes you can save a simple design by popping the air bubble that prevents the sheet from making contact with the color.

12-3

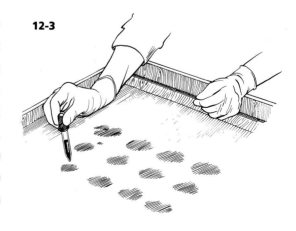

When your entire paper has made contact with the color, lift it out of the marbling tray and place it on layers of newspaper. Blot any excess beads of paint with a paper towel, and remove it to a drying area.

Skim excess color from the water before making another print.

■

MARBLING WITH A SIZE

Marbling on a size will give you more pattern control than marbling on water. We like to use carrageenan moss, available from a marbling supplier, but a size made from methyl cellulose can also be used. Liquid starch, wallpaper paste, and cornstarch are other size possibilities to explore.

In addition to the equipment noted above, you'll also need a large pot for mixing the size, and a rinse board and bucket or nearby sink to facilitate rinsing the excess size from printed papers. A gallon (4L) jug or hose can be used to dispense the water.

*M*AKING A METHYL CELLULOSE SIZE

A basic methyl cellulose recipe consists of mixing about 4 tablespoons (75ml) into about 6 pints (3l) of water. Let the mixture stand for about 15 minutes, until it becomes clear and smooth, before pouring it into your tray, skimming off bubbles, and applying paints. A general rule is to use a size about the

consistency of milk, but it's fun to play with thicker or thinner sizes to see how the paints react to them.

Note: Although we've never experienced this problem, some marblers have used a type of methyl cellulose that won't dissolve unless it's mixed in alkaline water. If you have difficulty getting the methyl cellulose to dissolve, try adding 2 tablespoons (25ml) of ammonia to the size and stirring until the mixture looks clear. Then add 2 tablespoons (25ml) of white vinegar and stir the mixture to render it neutral again and ready to place in your marbling tray.

*M*AKING CARRAGEENAN BLENDER SIZE

To make this type of size, you'll mix about 2 tablespoons (25ml) of instant powdered carrageenan with 1 gallon (4L) of water. First measure out the amounts of water and powdered carrageenan you'll need, then add enough water to half fill your blender and turn the setting to low. (Since carrageenan is a food additive, you needn't worry about contaminating your kitchen blender.) When the water is in motion, slowly sprinkle in 1 scant tablespoon (15ml) of size and blend for several seconds to dissolve the powder. Then add enough water to bring the blender to three-quarters full and blend another minute before pouring the mixture into a waiting pot or bucket.

Repeat this process until you've mixed all the size with the water. If you let the mixture stand overnight, most of the bubbles introduced by blending will dissipate. But you can use blender size for oil marbling immediately after making it if you spend some time skimming off the bubbles.

12-4

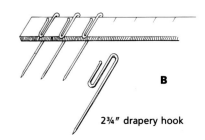

2¾″ drapery hook

■ **FIGURE 12-4.**

A. *Styrofoam or balsa wood that's ½ inch (1.3cm) thick makes a good base material for a marbling comb. Cut a strip ¾ to 1 inch (1.9 to 2.5cm) wide and slightly shorter than the length of your marbling tray. Draw a line lengthwise down the center of the strip and mark it off in ¼- or ½-inch (6mm or 1.3cm) increments to help position the comb teeth. Then push in long T-pins or nonrusting dressmaker's pins. To pattern colors in a vertical direction, make another comb slightly shorter than the width of your tray.*

B. *To make a simple rake, cut a ¼ inch (6mm) thick strip of balsa, pine, or foam core slightly longer than the length of your tray and slip drapery hooks over it at regular intervals. If the rake teeth are at least an inch (2.5cm) apart, they can work around the edges of the marbling tray and the rake can be used vertically as well as horizontally.*

■

MARBLING ON A SIZE

You can use a hair pick, a piece of broom straw, or a toothpick to pattern oil colors floating on a size. Rakes made by slipping drapery pins over a piece of molding, and combs made by pushing pins through a length of balsa wood, also make good patterning tools. The oil patterns will show the influence of combing movements in their soft-edged designs. Tiny beads of oil paint will often stipple a combed print, adding to its unique appearance. Suggestions for making some simple combed designs follow. (Many additional patterns and experimental designs are explained in detail in *Marbling,* listed in the bibliography.)

FINAL STEP: DRYING

After making your marbled print, rinse off any excess size clinging to it and blot off any excess color accumulation. Then dry the print on layers of newspaper, drying racks, or lines. If you string lengths of 3-inch (7.5cm) PVC pipe over the lines, your papers will dry without the crimp in the middle that clothesline often imparts. Most dry papers can be flattened by placing them under a board or heavy books. Any problem sheets can be ironed between sheets of paper. Flattened papers can be used in various paper projects, or marbled a second time to create more complex multiple-image patterns.

■ *This is an example of multiple-image oil-color marbling. Color was applied to a carrageenan size with a whisk. The sheet was dried and then re-marbled using the same technique with different colors.*

12-5

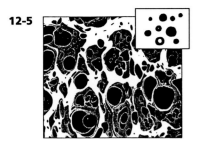
A

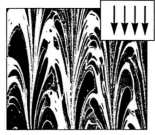
B

C

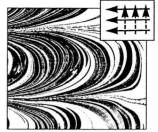
D

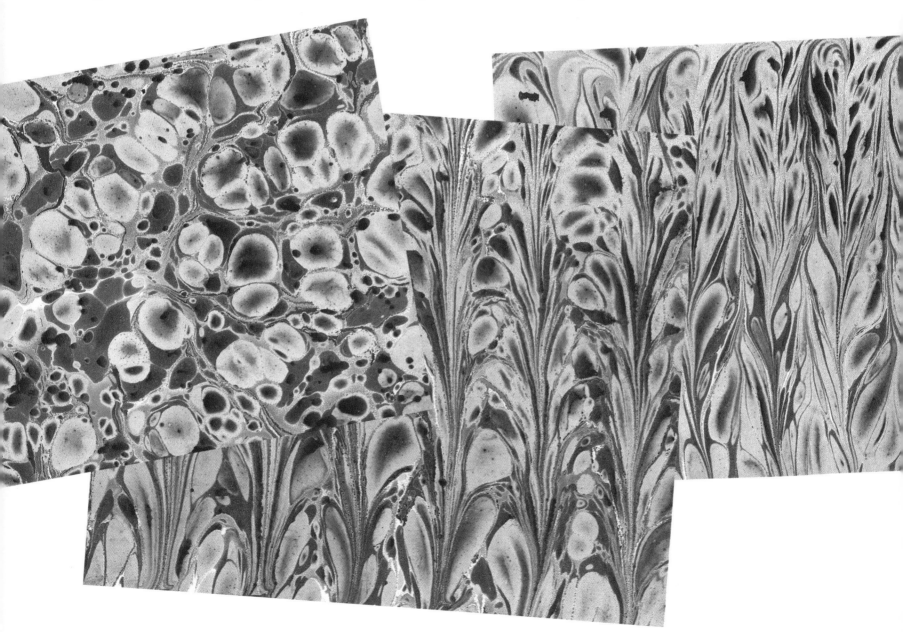

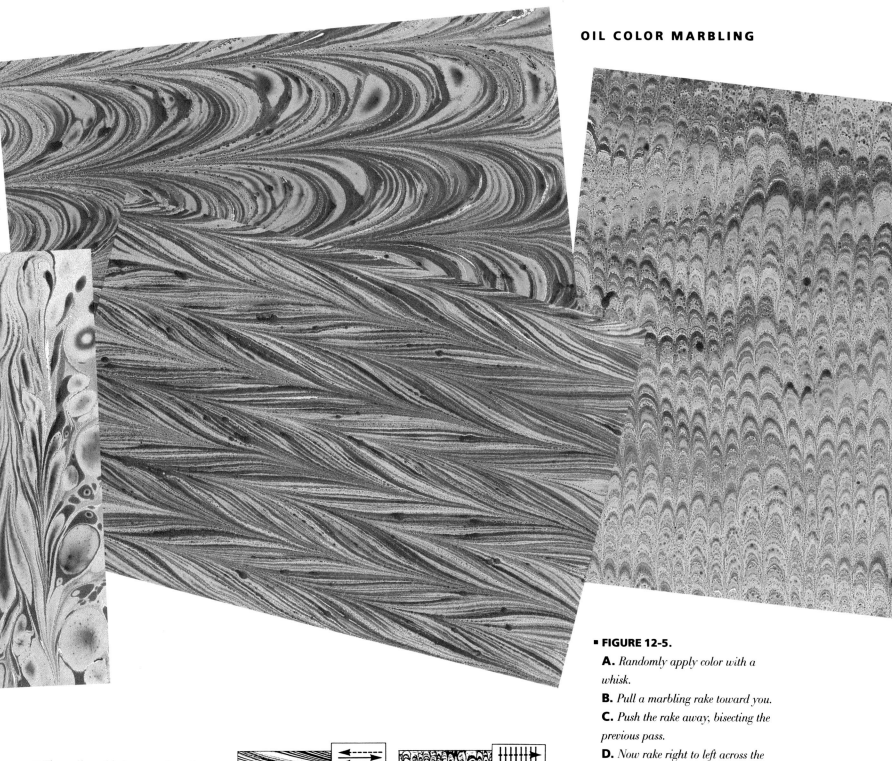

These oil marbled papers show the results of the following steps A through F.

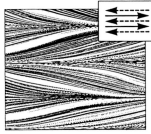

E

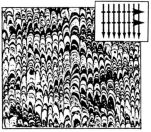

F

■ FIGURE 12-5.

A. *Randomly apply color with a whisk.*

B. *Pull a marbling rake toward you.*

C. *Push the rake away, bisecting the previous pass.*

D. *Now rake right to left across the grain.*

E. *Rake left to right bisecting the previous pass.*

F. *Pull a ¼-inch (6mm) comb (or one that is larger) toward you for a variation of a nonpareil pattern.*

Paper PROJECTS

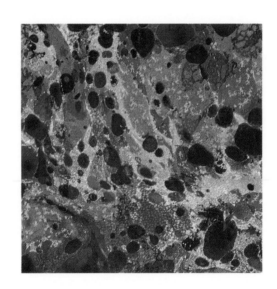

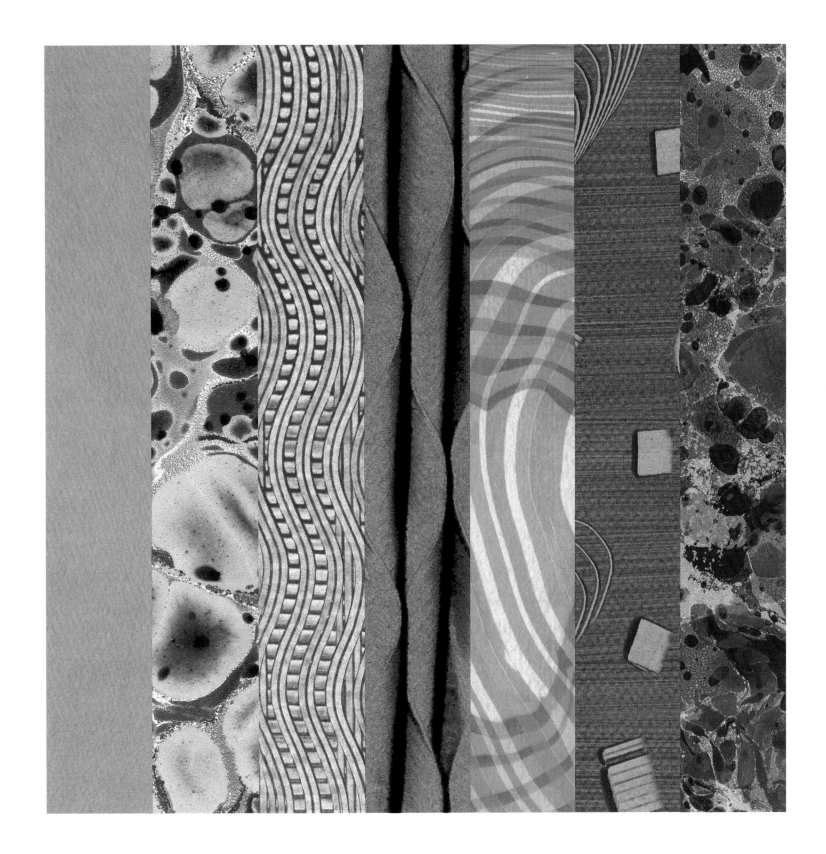

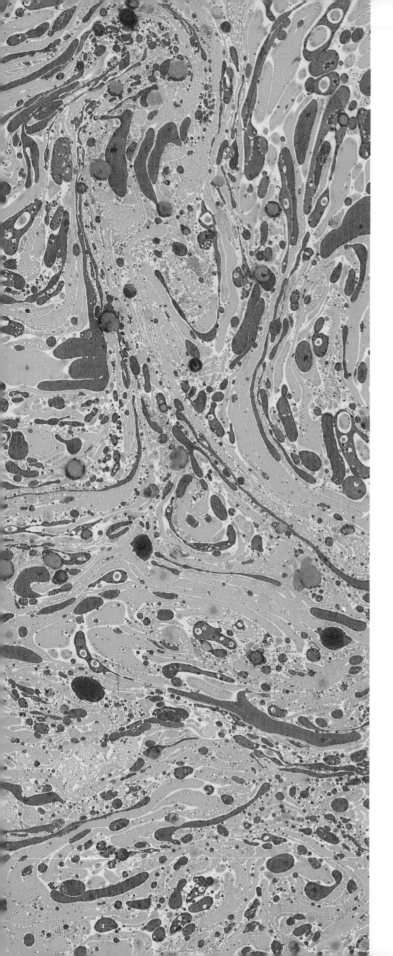

Working with Paper and Mat Board

By now you've probably experimented with some of the paper-decorating techniques described and have a neat stack of gorgeous papers ready to be transformed into delightful treasures for your own use, or to serve as unique gifts.

If you're raring to go, and simply must make something right away, do this: cut a piece of mat board, cover it with decorated paper, tie a string through it, glue a notepad to it, write "Do Not Disturb" on the top sheet, and hang the whole thing on the outside of your door. Then come back and read a bit more. A number of simple procedures are explained in this chapter to help you make attractive, professional-looking projects. None of them are difficult or very time consuming, but doing them correctly can often help you produce work that finds a permanent resting place on the mantel, instead of in the dresser drawer. Practice the following procedures on some scrap paper and board before attempting them in projects.

■

TECHNIQUES

Bonding Papers

There are a number of adhesives available today, such as the spray adhesive called Spray Mount made by 3M, and the adhesive release paper Cello-Mount. Using these will make projects easier but may also produce a weaker bond. Use your judgment; if your goal is to produce projects that achieve heirloom status, stick with liquid glues like Sobo and Elmer's or use "Yes" paste.

If you're spreading liquid glue over a large area, work quickly to prevent one section of the paper from drying while you work on the others. Work over a sheet of scrap paper when applying glue, and starting at the center and working toward the edges, spread the glue evenly over the entire surface of the paper or board.

To produce good results, follow manufacturers' directions when working with alternative adhesives.

■ **OPPOSITE PAGE:** *Oil marbling on carrageenan size by Jennifer Philippoff. The original is 11 by 17 inches (28 x 43cm).*

Burnishing

Smoothing, or burnishing, papers helps to sharpen a crease or fold and bond glued papers. It also helps to push out wrinkles and eliminate air bubbles trapped between glued papers and the boards they cover. To avoid damaging or shining the paper being burnished, cover it with a sheet of tracing paper. When working with glued sheets, hold the burnisher on its side and smooth from the center of the sheet outward to flatten it.

Cutting

Always be sure that you have a sharp blade in your mat knife or X-Acto knife before you attempt to cut boards and papers. To use a knife correctly, hold it in an upright position and slide it against a metal ruler as you cut. You'll need to make several cuts to separate chipboard or mat board.

Finding Paper Grain

Paper and chipboard, like fabric and wood, have what's known as a grain. Papers and boards that have become wet with glue will curl with the grain as they dry. It's important that the grains of both materials match when they're bonded, otherwise they'll curl in opposite directions during the drying process and produce a warped project.

To test for grain in a piece of paper, bend the sheet in half. If it collapses easily, you're bending with the grain. If it fights back, you're bending cross-grain. Mat board and chipboard will give you similar information about their grain directions when you attempt to bend them.

You'll minimize problems if you test papers and boards and mark them with an arrow showing grain direction before you begin using them in a project. Always make sure that their grains run vertically when you use them.

Mitering Corners

The ability to make tight, well-mitered corners is the mark of a good craftsperson. With a little practice, you'll be able to fold and fit papers together at the corners of boards they cover smoothly and rapidly. Then, when you glue them down, you'll produce a sharp, unwrinkled edge. Follow the diagrams pictured to practice this procedure.

Pressing

Papers that have been stretched by gluing will shrink as they dry and tend to warp the boards they cover. To prevent warping, place projects in a press, interleaved with wax paper where glue may seep out, and let them dry overnight.

Scoring

Scoring—using a pointed tool to help crease a paper's surface—will help you neatly fold heavy papers. To score, hold a metal rule on the fold line of a sheet, and using the rule as a guide, drag the point of an awl or large needle down the fold line. The object is to indent rather than break the surface of the paper. When you fold, fold away from, not into, the score line.

■

EQUIPMENT

Brushes

Large and small natural-bristle brushes that are stiff, yet flexible make good glue brushes. My favorites are a #6 and a #12 Gainsborough by M. Grumbacher.

Burnisher

A bookbinder's bone folder is the best burnishing tool. They're inexpensive and easy to find in arts-and-crafts catalogs. A tongue depressor or the back of a plastic comb is a workable substitute.

Cutting Mat

A self-healing cutting mat or a piece of glass with its sharp edges taped will protect your worktable when you score paper or divide paper and mat board with a knife. Don't try to cut on sheets of cardboard; it will only dull your knife blade.

Cutting Tools

A number of types of cutting tools will be needed for paper projects. For straight cutting you'll need an X-Acto or craft knife and a mat knife with a heavier blade. Good, sharp scissors will also be needed.

Metal Ruler

A metal ruler is essential if you don't have a steel square (even if you do, the ruler will still come in handy). Get one that's at least 18 inches (45cm) long, if possible.

Pressing Boards

Two heavy boards, or your paper press, will protect glued projects from warping as they dry.

Scoring Tool

An awl or weaving needle is needed for scoring thick papers to create a fold line and for perforating others.

Square

A T square, carpenter's square, or triangle will be needed for some projects to assure that paper corners are cut at right angles and edges of boards are perfectly straight.

Toothpicks

Toothpicks are ideal for depositing glue in those hard-to-reach places where a brush is too big to use safely.

13-1

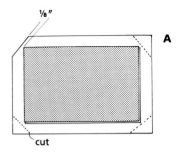

1/8" — cut — A

B

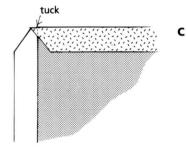

tuck — C

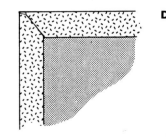

D

MATERIALS

■

Adhesive Release Paper

An alternative to gluing is to use one of the many adhesive release papers, like Positional Mounting Adhesive, to laminate papers to each other and to the various boards they'll cover in projects. This paper consists of a thin, double-sided adhesive sheet sandwiched between two protective papers. To use it, you peel away one protective sheet and apply the exposed adhesive to the wrong side of your decorative paper. When you peel away the other protective paper, you're left with a decorative sticky sheet that's ready to be used in a project.

Book Cloth

Book cloth or cloth tape (available at hardware stores) is used to hinge and decorate several projects. It is preferable to use book cloth or a cloth tape that is fabric rather than plastic.

Decorative Paper

Papers in various weights and thicknesses are needed to make these projects. Use cover-weight, text-weight, and thinner bond-weight papers.

Glue

Sobo glue, Elmer's glue, or "Yes" paste can be used to glue projects. "Yes" paste has the added benefit of not wrinkling papers even if they're very thin. Glue sticks are also useful when a small amount of glue is required. If you need to thin the glue, do so sparingly to maintain a good adhesive quality.

Graph Paper

Graph paper may help in positioning boards for laying out some of the projects.

Laminating Sheets

Clear plastic laminating sheets will be called for.

Mat Board

Mat board, chipboard, or binder's board can all serve as the light- to medium-weight board called for.

Plain Paper

Plain paper is used as a backing for decorative papers in many projects.

Poster Board

A few of the projects call for light two-ply mat board or poster board.

Scrap Paper

Newsprint and cast-off computer paper are placed under papers being glued and then discarded.

Spray Adhesive

Spray Mount is an alternative to gluing. It's especially useful when bonding sheets of paper together. Follow directions on the package carefully.

Tracing Paper

A thin sheet of tracing paper is placed between a bone folder and the paper being smoothed to prevent it from being damaged during burnishing or folding.

Waxed Paper

Waxed paper is used to prevent glue from one section of a project from ruining another during pressing.

■ **FIGURE 13-1.**

A. *To miter corners, first cut off the corners of the decorative cover papers, leaving about ⅛ inch (3mm) of space between the board and the paper.*

B. *Apply glue and fold the top flap down. Then glue the bottom flap down.*

C. *Tuck and fold the small overlaps of paper in toward the side flaps at each corner. These prevent the corners of your board from showing.*

D. *Fold and glue the side flaps to finish.*

CHAPTER 14

For the Home

Any number of paper projects can be made to decorate your home or to be given as memorable gifts to special friends. You'll probably think of lots of other uses for your papers as you work on these projects. If your tastes, like mine, are fairly eclectic, you won't have to concern yourself with creating papers designed to carry out a strictly Victorian or Southwestern theme. You will want to concern yourself with color, however, and also consider the size of the finished project when deciding the scale of the pattern you will use on a piece. A 3-inch (7.5cm) stencil of a rabbit, repeated every two inches (5cm), would be a ridiculous choice for a coaster paper. But a repeat stamping of a tiny star would be just as silly to use on a window shade. Not only would it take forever to do, but you'd barely be able to see it. The projects that follow will offer suggestions for using papers and patterns to advantage. Modify them to complement your decor.

WALLPAPER

Sandra Holzman's stunning oil-marbled wallpaper is made in a huge marbling tray filled with water. Her flowing designs are often complemented with stencil or rubber stamp printing. You may not want to tackle such a large marbling job, but stenciling or printing on plain wallpaper wouldn't be hard to do. (If you do want to try marbling on a grand scale, you can build a large makeshift tray by draping heavy plastic over a base constructed of two-by-fours.)

WINDOW TREATMENTS

Like wallpaper, purchased window shades can be decorated with marbled, stenciled, or printed designs. Plain or colored shades could be used. If you have some small, narrow windows, you may want to try suminagashi-marbling some heavy Japanese paper (available in rolls) and attaching it to a conventional shade apparatus.

You can also create a hanging screen by following these directions. Suminagashi-marble a length of

■ **OPPOSITE PAGE:** *This paper shows traditional suminagashi marbling.*
RIGHT: *These lengths of wallpaper by Sandra Holzman were oil-marbled on water. Sandra used stencil resists, rubber stamps, and acrylic paints to further decorate her papers.*

absorbent paper. You can use a large makeshift tray or marble your paper in sections, allowing one marbled area to overlap the next. After the paper is dry, press it and then hem it at the top and bottom by running a line of glue about 2½ inches (6.4cm) in from either end and folding the paper back into the glue. When the glue is dry, insert decorative curtain rods through the hemmed areas and attach them to your window frame. Use thin dowels if you prefer to make a hanging window screen. An orizomegami or tie-dyed paper would also make an attractive screen; when these papers are backlit, they look almost magical.

■

LAMPSHADES

Lampshades can be designed to coordinate with decorated wallpapers and window treatments. It's easy to print on a purchased hexagonal shade, but printing on a tapered shade can present problems. Sponge prints, however, are a snap. Cut and punctured shades are especially fun to make, and they can offer the added benefit of providing dramatic plays of light and shadow when they illuminate an otherwise dark room.

Our favorite, however, is a pleated shade, appropriate for any paper-decorating medium, or any decor for that matter. Ours was done using Unryu rice paper. Because the Japanese paper that we used was thin, we designed the shade to fit over a white purchased shade instead of over a lampshade frame. Some general directions follow; modify them to create any size shade you wish.

14-1

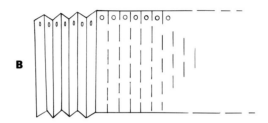

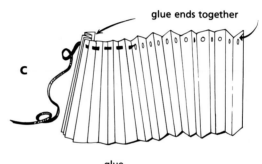

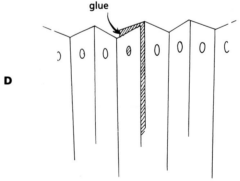

glue ends together

glue

For a shade with a 4-inch (10cm) top ring, a 10-inch (25cm) bottom ring, and a depth of 7 inches (17.5cm), decorate a piece of paper 52 inches (130cm) long and 8½ inches (21.3cm) wide. It's easiest to work with a roll of wallpaper or rice paper, but you can join paper sections with glue in the pleated areas if necessary.

■ **FIGURE 14-1.**

A. *Rule pleating lines on the wrong side of your paper and mark the spots where the ribbon holes will be punched.*

B. *Accordion-pleat the entire length of paper and punch the ribbon holes.*

C. *Thread your ribbon through the holes to gather the shade.*

D. *Overlap and glue the ends of the pleated paper so that your ribbon runs in a continuous circle through the top of the shade.*

■ *The rice paper for this pleated shade was suminagashi-marbled several times to produce the overlapping patterns and colors.*

Although simple accordion pleats create this shade, it's easy to misfold when you're doing so many in succession. To be safe, rule pleat lines on the wrong side of the decorative paper. Ours are 1 inch (2.5cm) apart. Instead of measuring for each line, cut a 1-inch (2.5cm) wide strip of mat board and lay it on each line to gauge where to mark the next.

When you've marked all the pleat lines, rule a long line across the top of the paper, ½ inch (1.3cm) down from the edge. This line will help position the ribbon holes. Accordion-fold the paper, and then punch a hole between each pleat on the line running across the top of the shade.

To gather the shade, overlap and glue the ends of the pleated paper and thread a ribbon through the holes. Place the shade over its support, adjust the pleats, and tie a decorative bow to finish the project.

■

PLACE MATS AND COASTERS

Very serviceable matching coasters and place mats are easy to make, and their patterns can be designed to coordinate with a particular dinner theme. A fish-print paper could liven up a seafood buffet, while a cactus stencil design or batik chili paper could be used to make place mats that are presented with a gift of Mexican condiments. (And paste papers, of course, could go with lots of dinners . . . especially spaghetti.)

For thin place mats and coasters, you can just decorate a cover stock, cut it to size, and sandwich it between clear contact paper or have it professionally laminated. (Most photocopy centers now do laminating.) Then simply trim the laminating film close to the decorative paper to finish.

To make a more substantial place mat or coaster, bond papers to a mat-board backing and cut them to size. Then coat them with an acrylic sealer or cover them with clear adhesive film.

A matching tray can easily be made by placing a sheet of decorative paper on a purchased tray and covering it with a sheet of glass or Plexiglas.

■

COASTER BOX

A matching box can be made to hold your decorated coasters. This box has sides that are 1¼ inches (3.1cm) high and is designed to hold 4- by 4-inch (10 x 10cm) coasters. The layout for the box will be 2¾ inches (7cm) longer and wider than the coasters to give the coasters some room in the box and to allow for the height of the sides. To make this box, draw a 6¾-inch (16.9cm) square on a piece of mat board, then rule and score a line 1¼ inches (3.1cm) in on all four sides. Cut out the corners formed by the intersecting lines and fold the box sides up. Glue or tape the sides in place and prepare the cover papers.

There are several ways to cover a box. The simplest way is to just place the box on an oversized square of paper and bring up the sides, folding them in as though you were wrapping a package. The results, however, aren't very professional looking. The directions that follow will allow you to cover this box and other ready-made boxes neatly and professionally. It

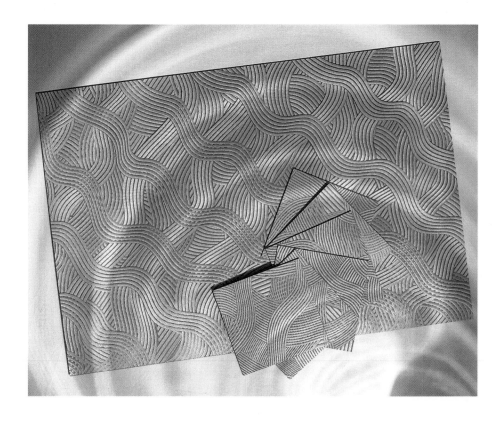

may be easiest for you to first work on graph paper and try it on your box before gluing up your decorated paper.

Begin by tracing around the bottom of your box. Then draw the sides of the box by laying it on its sides and tracing around them. If you're constructing a box, of course, you can do this before you tape the sides up. Extend each of these sides by the box height plus ¼ inch (6mm), as shown in figure 14-3. This added length will allow you to wrap the paper up over the outside of the box, down the inside wall of the box, and ¼ inch (6mm) onto the box floor.

To avoid producing a covered box with corners that peek out, you'll have to add little flaps (E) to two opposing sides of the paper, as shown. These will cover the box corners where the papers join and will also help hold the box together.

■ *The "spaghetti" paste-paper design that covers this set of place mats and coasters was drawn with calligraphy pens. The decorative papers were mounted on heavy mat board to give them a rigid backing.*

After you've drawn the appropriate pattern on your decorated paper, cut it out and fold on all the lines. Glue the bottom of the box in place and then glue the sides with the flaps in place. After the last sides are glued in place, cut and glue in a liner to cover the bottom of the box.

You can make a box lid in a similar way, starting with a larger base square and making shorter sides. Existing boxes can be covered by modifying the directions given here.

■ **FIGURE 14-2.**

A. *To begin the coaster box, rule and score the appropriate lines on a piece of mat board and cut away the corners where the lines intersect.*
B. *Fold the box sides up and tape them in place while you prepare the cover papers.*

■ **FIGURE 14-3.** *The pattern for the box covering consists of a central area the size of the box base, and four sides that are twice the height of the box plus ¼ inch (6mm).*

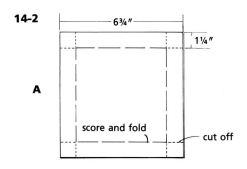

14-2

6¾"

1¼"

A

score and fold

cut off

B

tape

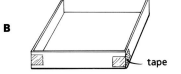

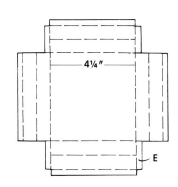

14-3

4¼"

E

A BOX FOR PLAYING CARDS OR PHOTOS

A box to hold playing cards or photos can be constructed using the same techniques you followed to make the coaster box. The card box has a 4- by 5-inch (10 x 12.5cm) base and ⅞-inch (2.2cm) tall sides, and is designed to be glued into a companion case. The case, which is made exactly like a book cover, functions as a base and fold-down cover for the box.

To make the case for the card box, cut two pieces of mat board each 4½ by 5½ inches (11.3 x 13.8cm). These will become the cover and the base of the case. Cut another piece 1 by 5½ inches (2.5 x 13.8cm) long to become the spine of the case. Position the boards on a piece of decorative cloth tape (or glued book cloth) that's 2 inches (5cm) wide and 6½ inches (16.3cm) long, as shown in figure 14-4. Make sure the tops of the boards are even and a ⅛-inch (3mm) margin is left between the spine and the other boards. Fold the tape over the boards to attach them. Now apply a 2- by 5¼-inch (5 x 13.1cm) strip of book tape to neatly cover the inside of the spine. Use a bone folder to burnish the tape down and crease it into the ⅛-inch (3mm) grooves on either side of the spine. Turn the case over and crease the tape into the grooves on the front of case.

Now it's time to cover the case with decorated paper. Begin by cutting two 5- by 6½-inch (12.5 x 16.3cm) pieces of paper. When these are applied to the boards, they'll overlap the cloth tape by about ¼ inch (6mm) and extend about ½ inch (1.3cm) beyond the top, bottom, and front (fore edge) of the boards. You may want to rule a line ¼ inch (6mm) in from the edge of the cloth tape to help position the decorated paper.

Bond the papers to the boards, burnishing them down carefully. Then miter the corners of the paper and fold them toward the inside of the case. Glue down the top and bottom edges first; then glue the remaining long edge down. (You can apply glue directly to the boards, burnish the paper down, and then glue down the folded edges, or coat your entire paper with adhesive and apply it to the dry board. Use whatever method is easiest for you.)

Now cut two 4¼- by 5¼-inch (10.6 x 13.1cm) pieces of decorated paper to line the inside of the case. These will overlap the cloth tape by ¼ inch (6mm) and cover the paper edges you just glued down. Twelve-inch (30cm) ribbon ties may be added at this point, if desired. Glue a 3-inch (7.5cm) section of each ribbon into the center of each board before you apply the liner papers. Burnish and press the open case overnight if using liquid adhesive. When the case is dry, glue the card box to one side of it.

14-4

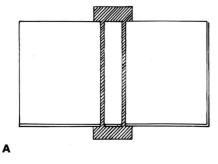

A

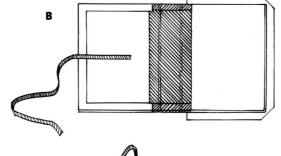

B

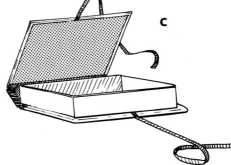

C

■ **FIGURE 14-4.**

A. *Position the case boards on a piece of glued book cloth, making sure the tops of the boards are even and ⅛-inch (3mm) margins are left between the spine and the adjoining boards.*

B. *Bond the decorative papers to the case boards so that they overlap the book cloth by about ¼ inch (1.3cm). Then miter the corners of the papers and fold them toward the inside of the case.*

C. *When you have applied the ribbons and lined the case, glue the card box to one side of it.*

■ **OPPOSITE PAGE:** *This card box was made with oil-marbled papers and satin ribbon ties.* **BELOW:** *Hair picks were used to create the design on this paste-paper picture mat, which was created to complement a wicker dresser.*

■

A STANDING PICTURE MAT

It's a rare person who doesn't have a few photos tucked away in an album that could bring a lot more enjoyment if they were put on display. Or perhaps a special drawing could use a complementary decorative mat. A yellow sponge-print paper resembling Swiss cheese became the perfect mat for a small watercolor painting I was given. It now hangs in the kitchen, close to the floor above the food bowl of my cat, Murphy. The subject? Three blind mice. Although hanging mice are nice, the mat made by the following directions is not a wall piece; it's designed to stand on a mantel or shelf, becoming both the mat and the frame for a photo or drawing.

You can begin with a purchased 5- by 7-inch (12.5 x 17.5cm) mat or make your own. To make your own mat, cut a 5- by 7-inch (12.5 x 17.5cm) piece of mat board and rule lines 1¼ inch (3.1cm) from the top and bottom edges of the board, as shown in figure 14-5. Rule two more lines 1 inch (2.5cm) in from the sides of the board. Then cut out the 3- by 4½-inch (7.5 x 11.3cm) window formed by these intersecting lines. This gives you a mat with top and bottom borders of 1¼ inches (3.1cm) and sides of 1 inch (2.5cm); it is designed to hold a 3½- by 5-inch (9 x 12.5cm) photo.

Cover the mat with a piece of decorative paper cut 1 inch (2.5cm) larger than the mat all around. Begin by applying adhesive to the front of the mat to be covered, and then center it on the decorative paper. (You may want to draw some guidelines for positioning the mat before you apply the glue to make it easier to center.) Cut, fold, and glue the windowed area as shown, wrapping it tightly to create a mat opening that's square, not misshapen. Fold and glue the paper around the outside of the mat, too, burnishing it down and making well-mitered corners.

To make the backing for the mat, cut another 5- by 7-inch (12.5 x 17.5cm) piece of mat board and cover it with decorative paper, too, burnishing the paper to smooth it down. Then cut another piece of decorative paper slightly smaller than 5 by 7 inches (12.5 x 17.5cm) to cover the edges of the paper you just applied on the reverse side of the mat.

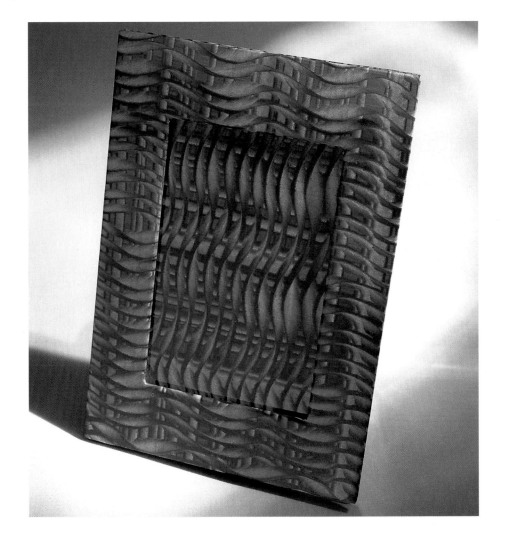

14-5

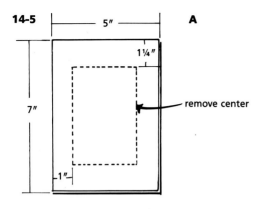

A

5"

1¼"

7"

remove center

1"

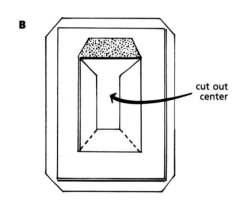

B

cut out center

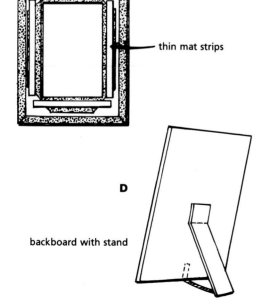

C

thin mat strips

D

backboard with stand

If you're using a liquid adhesive, you'll need to press both pieces until dry. (Put waxed paper between them if you stack them in the press.)

Thin pieces of mat board will keep the photo from slipping within the mat. Cut three strips of mat board, each ½ inch (1.3cm) by 4½ inches (11.3cm) long. Glue these to the bottom and side edges of the back of the windowed mat, leaving about ⅜ inch (10mm) of space between them and the edge of the window to accommodate the picture borders.

To make a mat stand, cut a piece of board 1 by 4½ inches (2.5 x 11.3cm); score it 1 inch (2.5cm) down from the top so that it can bend enough to support the mat. Cover the piece of board with a decorative paper, and glue the inch-long (2.5cm) section to the mat back. Attach a decorative ribbon between the bottom of the stand and the mat.

Now glue the other papered board to the strips to join the front and back sections of the picture mat. The top is left open so a photo and protective sheet of clear acetate can be slipped in.

▪ FIGURE 14-5.

A. *Rule the top, bottom, and side borders for your mat and remove the center of the mat where the lines intersect.*

B. *Glue your decorative paper to the mat. Then cut, fold, and glue the windowed area, wrapping it tightly toward the back of the mat to create an opening that is square.*

C. *Miter the corners of the decorative paper and fold and glue these around the back of the mat. Add three mat-board or double-sided foam-tape strips to create a space for the photo between the mat and its backing.*

D. *Glue the stand to the backboard, attaching the ribbon support to the back of the mat before joining the mat to its backing.*

▪

THE CANDLE LANTERN

This beautiful lantern was designed by Jeff Mathison to cover one of the battery-operated candles so popular at Christmastime. The soft, romantic light that shines through the rice-paper windows makes it a year-round favorite, useful on a buffet or bookshelf. Although it can't be used over an actual candle, it can be used over a small electric lamp.

■ **FIGURE 14-6.**

A. *To form the lantern base, cut a piece of mat board 10 by 18 inches (25 x 45cm). (This measurement includes the ½-inch [1cm] flap of paper that holds the structure together.) Score and fold the mat board every 3½ inches (8.8cm). Then make a stencil for the window design, trace it onto the mat board, and cut the windows out. Attach decorative paper behind the window openings before gluing the structure together.*

B. *Make the roof by dividing a 9-inch (22.5cm) diameter circle of mat board into six pie-shaped wedges. Then remove one of the sections, leaving the flap of paper pictured. When attached to the previous wedge, it will hold the roof in position. Another way to make this structure would be to form one equilateral triangle and use it as a pattern to create the roof design.*

■ **RIGHT:** *Thin rice paper bearing an orizomegami design created the stained glass windows for our lantern. Suminagashi-marbled paper would also be a good choice for window material.*

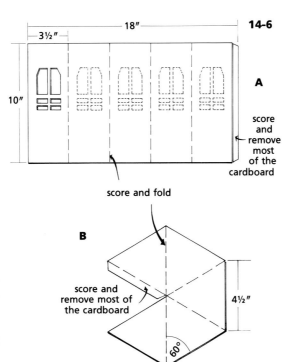

14-6

score and remove most of the cardboard

score and fold

score and remove most of the cardboard

This lantern is 10 inches (25cm) tall and is composed of five 3½-inch (8.8cm) mat-board walls with identical cutout windows. The roof consists of five triangles, each 5½ inches (13.8cm) tall, with a 4½-inch (11.3cm) base. Both the roof and the base of the lantern were constructed from single boards. They were deeply scored at intervals, as shown, to facilitate folding. When the mat board was being cut away, a flap was left on the roof and base, to be used later to glue the structure together. A strip of book tape could be applied to the inside of the lantern instead if you have difficulty creating these flaps.

A stencil of the window design was made, and the pattern was traced on each panel. Then a mat knife was used to carefully cut out each windowpane. A tiny orizomegami paper was used to line each of the window openings. Then the lantern base and the roof were each glued together.

The lantern was originally designed to be covered with a decorated paper, but the scored mat board was so elegant that we decided to leave it stark white and focus attention on the rice-paper windows. Use your stencil-cutting skills to make a similar lantern with your own design for the windows. Two-ply mat board isn't difficult to cut. And there's a bonus: the stencil that's used to make the window design can be used to create several types of note cards. We did a cutout windowed card, a stenciled version, and an embossed one using a repeat of the window design.

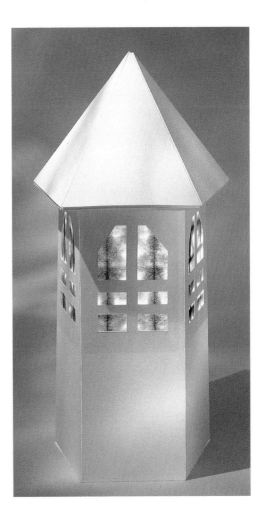

CHAPTER 15

For the Office

A lot of the people I've spoken with lately seem to be preoccupied with the same thing—getting organized. As we all get more busy, our desks get more cluttered, and more time is spent looking for a stray paper clip, rubber band, or receipt that didn't make it into the filing cabinet before the telephone rang. The projects in this chapter are designed to help you or your friends organize the workplace or home office—and do it beautifully.

- **FIGURE 15-1.** *After you've glued and wrapped a matching decorative paper around your matchboxes, arrange them on the wrong side of your mat-board square.*

- **OPPOSITE PAGE:** *A multicolored pulp "Rugg Road Special" hand-made paper.* **BELOW:** *Wooden alphabet stamps and some random objects found lurking in our junk drawer were inked and stamped to create the papers for this fastener box. Baby buttons, shaped like pencils, were used as drawer pulls.*

THE FASTENER BOX

Wayward pushpins, staples, paper clips, or rubber bands can be corralled and neatly housed on your desk in this attractive little four-drawered box. It's easily created by sandwiching four little matchboxes between two paper-covered squares of mat board.

To make a box like the one pictured, purchase some little matchboxes that are 1¼ by ¾ by 2 inches (3 x 2 x 5cm). Cover the cardboard sleeves with some decorated paper. Cut two 4-inch (10cm) squares of mat board and cover one side of each with matching pieces of decorative paper. Remove the little cardboard drawers from the matchboxes, and using felt-

15-1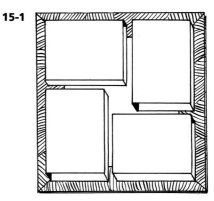

tip markers or acrylics, paint them a color that matches your decorated paper. Add drawer-pulls by stitching a baby button onto the front and the back of each drawer front. (The hidden button will prevent the thread from ripping through the thin box material.) You can also reinforce with a piece of cloth tape if you prefer.

Glue the four matching box sleeves to the bottom square, as shown, covering the edges of the paper you applied to the board and allowing about ¼ inch (6mm) margin around the matchboxes. When the sleeves are dry, insert the box drawers and glue the top in place. *Voilà!* You could make a matchbox tower this way.

THE POSTCARD FOLIO

Dropping a postcard to clients or friends when a thought occurs is a good way to keep up with correspondence. And keeping a stack of postcards handy will help you accomplish this. The postcard folio is made just like the playing card case (see page 95). This, too, is really a book cover in disguise.

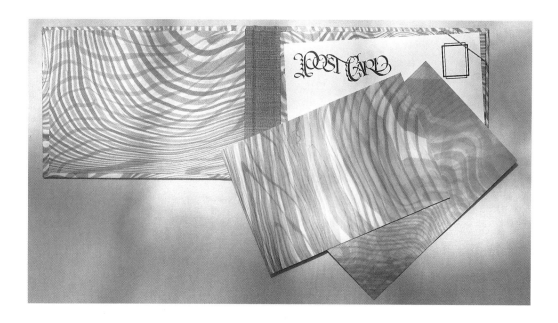

■ **LEFT:** *The postcard folio and accompanying postcards were made with suminagashi-marbled papers.*

■ **FIGURE 15-2.**

A. *The postcard folio is made exactly like the playing card case pictured in figure 14-4.*

B. *Wrap elastic braid around two edges of the paper-covered mat board and tie it at the back of the piece. Then glue the structure in place on the right-hand side of the folio.*

The folio boards are each 4½- by 6½-inch (11.3 x 16.3cm) pieces of mat board. They're separated by a 4½- by ½-inch (11.3 x 1.3cm) mat-board spine that has an ⅛-inch (3mm) space on either side of it. (If your board is heavier than standard mat board, you may have to leave a space that's a bit larger.)

Apply a 2-inch (5cm) wide strip of book tape to hinge the three pieces, as with the playing card case, and then apply cover papers and liners. Press the open folio if using a liquid glue.

Now cut another 4¼- by 6¼-inch (10.6 x 15.6cm) piece of mat board and cover it with a matching piece of decorated paper. Then take a piece of heavy elastic thread or thin elastic braid, wrap it around opposing corners of the board as shown, and tie it in a small flat knot at the back of the board. Glue that piece in place on the right-hand side of the folio. Press again. When the folio is dry, you just slip purchased postcards under the elastic corners. Or better yet, make your own postcards.

15-2

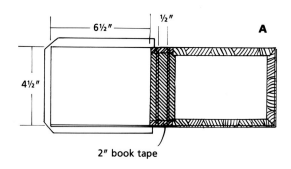
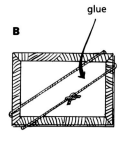

6½″

½″

4½″

A

B

glue

2″ book tape

■

POSTCARDS

You can use many of your decorated papers, even ornate handmade ones, alone or in a collage to create your own personal postcards. To make your postcard stock, use a spray adhesive like Spray Mount (follow precautions) or adhesive release paper

■ *The oil-marbled message station and orizomegami clipboard, ready for use.*

to bond a large sheet of decorated paper to a sheet of posterboard. Then cut your bonded paper into 4- by 6-inch (10 x 15cm) pieces to make postcards. You can decorate the plain side of the card and give it an official look by using your rubber stamping or printing skills to create an ornate center line and decorated postage stamp area.

■

A HANGING MESSAGE STATION

A message pad designed to hang near the telephone is less likely to be carried off or buried under the day's mail. This message station can also be posted outside your office door for clients to leave a note if they miss you. Our message station is designed to hold a 4- by 6-inch (10 x 15cm) purchased notepad. The mat board to which it's attached measures 6 by 9 inches (15 x 22.5cm).

To make a message station this size, cut a piece of decorative paper 7 by 10 inches (17.5 x 25cm) and bond it to the mat board, mitering the corners well. Press overnight if using liquid glue. Then punch two holes 2¼ inches (5.6cm) in from either side and ¾ inch (1.9cm) down from the top of the board. Thread ribbon through these holes, knotting and trimming it at the front of the message station, to create the ribbon hanger.

To make the pencil holder, punch two holes 2¼ inches (5.6cm) in from either side and 1 inch (2.5cm) up from the bottom of the piece. Cut two 2-inch (5cm) lengths of ribbon, and using a pencil as a guide to determine the loop size, insert both ends of a piece of ribbon into each hole. Open out the ribbon at the back of the mat board and glue each end of it down, leaving the pencil in place until dry.

Now attach the notepad between the ribbon decorations. Use thin strips of Velcro to mount the notepad. Then apply a backing sheet, and add a pencil that matches the ribbon or wrap one in decorative paper to match the message station.

CLIPBOARD

A noteworthy clipboard can be constructed in a matter of minutes. First decide what size notepad you'd like to use. Lined pads come in all sizes and colors; you can easily find something to coordinate with one of your decorated papers. Add 2 inches (5cm) to the height and 2½ inches (6.3cm) to the width of the notepad you choose. Then cut a piece of heavy chipboard to those dimensions, and cover the board, front and back, with decorated paper. (Glue two lighter boards together to make a heavy one, if necessary.) Finally add a purchased bulldog clip to hold the notepad to the decorative clipboard.

ACCORDION FILES

Expanding files, popular for holding checks and recipes, can be transformed from handy but homely organizers to beautiful objects you'd be proud to display.

Begin by cutting two pieces of mat board ½ inch (1.3cm) longer and wider than the standing file you wish to transform. Choose a piece of decorated paper that coordinates with the color of the file you're working on; the front and back will be hidden, but the top and the sides will be exposed. Cover the mat board with the decorated paper according to the directions on page 87, mitering, burnishing, and pressing the board if necessary. If your expanding file has cloth ties or a fold-over flap, neatly cut these off.

Ribbon ties in an appropriate color and width should now be cut. They should be long enough to tie in a large bow over a full file. Glue a ribbon about one third of the way down the center of the outside front and back of the file. When they're dry, glue the front decorative board over the ribbon. Insert a book in the file behind the decorative board to give it support until it's dry in case the file flexes too much. When the front board is dry, bond the other one to the back of the file over the second ribbon to finish.

■ *Batik papers by Jennifer Philippoff were used to decorate these purchased file envelopes.*

■ **FIGURE 15-3.**

A. *Glue the decorative paper to the pocket board, folding one flap under as shown.*

B. *Fold the decorative paper around the edges of the pocket board.*

C. *Glue the edges down at the back of the blotter.*

15-3

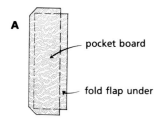

A

pocket board

fold flap under

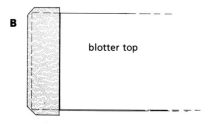

B

blotter top

C

blotter back

■ *Complementary oil-marbled papers, created on a carrageenan size, were used to create this desk blotter and accessory station.*

■

A DESK BLOTTER

Desk blotters come in all sizes. Some have triangular corners, while others have rectangular pockets at either end. Ours is 15 by 20 inches (37.5 x 50cm), with rectangular pockets that measure 3 by 15 inches (7.5 x 37.5cm). To make a blotter this size, first cut a mat-board base and pocket boards in the above dimensions. Then cut and bond a 17- by 17-inch (42.5 x 42.5cm) piece of blotter paper to the midsection of the base. (The exposed edges will be covered by the side pockets.)

Now cut two 5- by 17-inch (12.5 x 42.5cm) pieces of decorative paper to cover the pocket boards. Bond each pocket board to the center of each decorated sheet and fold and glue one long flap down. (The other three flaps will be used to mount the pocket to the blotter base.) If using glue, press all pieces before assembling the desk blotter.

To mount the pockets on the blotter base, clip the flap corners to miter them, and position the pockets on the base. Prefold the three flaps that extend from the pocket board to gauge how they'll fit around the blotter base. Then glue these flaps around the edges of the blotter base to attach the pockets.

Attach a sheet of heavy paper or felt to cover the bottom of the blotter. A lovely way to finish the project is to slip some blotter or handmade sheets, perhaps some that coordinate with the blotter itself, under the blotter pockets.

■

ACCESSORY STATION

The simplest way to make a pencil cup is, of course, to just cover a juice can. If that seems a bit undersized for your needs, however, you can make an accessory station that is capable of holding pencils, pens, scissors, brushes, and even flowers by covering sections of wide or narrow mailing tubes. Our station has three sections and was cut from one tube. A triangular piece of mat board creates a base for them.

You can leave all the tubes the same height or cut them to slightly different heights for another type of grouping. Cover each tube with decorative paper, folding it over the top of the tube to cover part of the inside as well. You can further decorate the tubes with book-tape trim or add decorative paper triangles to coordinate with a matching desk blotter. Finally, glue the tubes together and to a mat board base to create the accessory station.

■

SINGLE-SIGNATURE BOOKS

These little books can help you organize your thoughts by giving you a place to jot down ideas or make lists. Most books composed of several signatures are very time-consuming to make. But these books, composed of one section, are so simple to make that you can constantly renew them. You can make several: one for project ideas, one for appoint-

ments, perhaps another for shopping lists. You could even make cover papers to coordinate with each book's use, so you'll always reach for the right one.

To make a 4½- by 6½-inch (11.3 x 16.3cm) book with 24 pages, cut twelve 6- by 8-inch (15 x 20cm) pieces of plain paper. Fold each in half and arrange them in a folded stack. On the center fold line, make a light pencil mark at the 3-inch (7.5cm) center mark, and ¾ inch (1.9cm) in from either end.

Now cut a 4½- by 13-inch (11.3 x 32.5cm) decorative cover paper and fold it in half. Position the stack of plain paper inside the cover sheet so that the top and bottom margins are even. Then, using an awl or large needle, puncture the pages and cover of the book at the penciled marks.

Thread a large embroidery needle with a 20-inch (50cm) piece of embroidery floss or carpet thread in a color that coordinates with your cover paper and sew the book together as follows.

Starting at the inside of the book, bring the needle through the central hole (1) to the outside of the book, leaving about a 3-inch (7.5cm) tail of thread remaining inside. Now enter hole number 2, and carry the thread back to the inside of the book. Bypass the center hole and carry the thread all the way over to hole number 3. Enter that to reach the outside of the book again. Then come back through hole number 1 to the inside to rejoin the tail of thread that's been awaiting your return. Tie the thread attached to the needle to this 3-inch (7.5cm) strand, trapping the length of thread extending from hole number 2 to hole number 3 between the two short threads as you knot them.

Congratulations! You're now a bookmaker. Clip the ends of the knotted threads to finish.

15-4

A

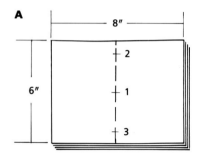

B

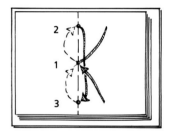

■ **FIGURE 15-4.**
A. *Mark and puncture your cover sheet and stack of pages to prepare them for stitching.*
B. *Stitch your book together by carrying your thread in the direction shown by the arrows. Be sure to trap the length of thread extending between point 2 and point 3 between the loose tails of thread when you knot them together.*

You can modify these directions to make more decorative books. If you begin sewing on the outside, for instance, and leave a longer tail, you can finish on the outside and tie the book together with a bow that cascades down the spine. You could also begin with a wider cover, and fold in front and back flaps (like a dust jacket) so decorative paper is visible on the inside of the book, as well. A decorative endpaper, perhaps a piece of your handmade paper, could be substituted for the first sheet of plain paper in the book, or the entire interior of the book could be composed of beautiful handmade sheets.

■ *These single-signature books were made with paste and oil-marbled papers. The decorative paper used for the train schedule was patterned with a calligraphy pen, a plastic spackle knife, and paste-covered cardboard. The domino book is a collage of oil-marbled papers with punched paper dots.*

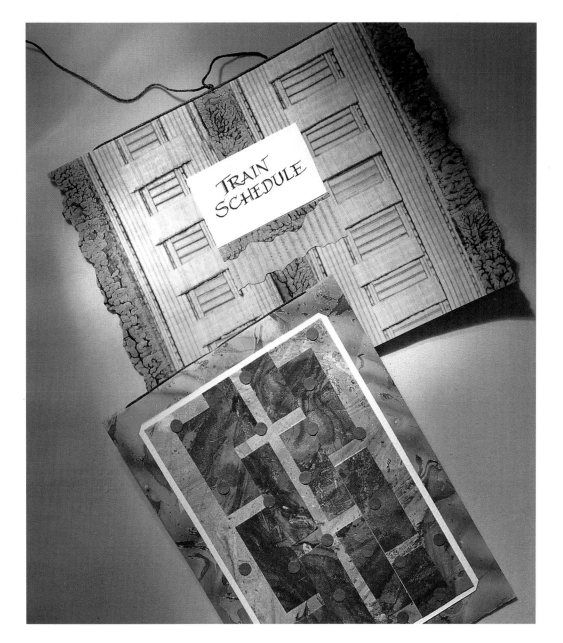

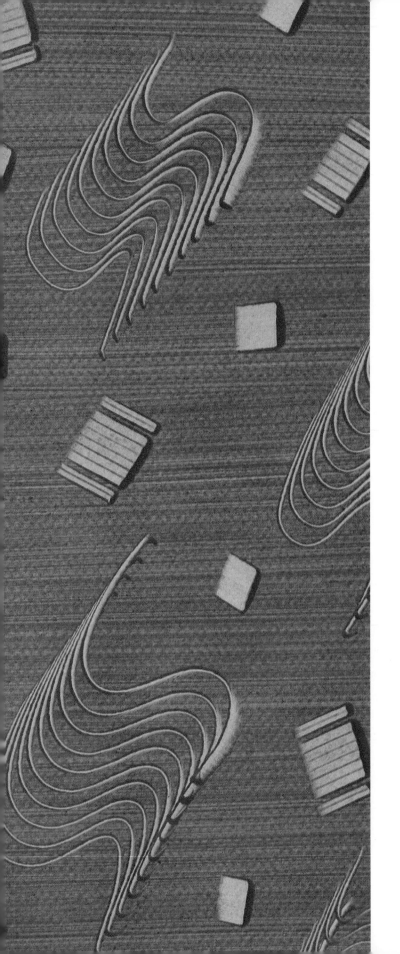

$\mathcal{F}$or Celebrations

$\mathcal{T}$here are lots of gorgeous greeting cards on the market today, but none of them can rival one that you've lovingly created with the receiver in mind. Hand-decorated wrapping papers, too, will be saved and admired long after the expensive commercial ones have been balled up and discarded. It's rewarding to watch someone who usually tears into their packages with gusto gingerly peel tape from a handmade sheet. Hand-crafted boxes are really showstoppers as well. In fact, you may have to upgrade your gifts if you don't want them to be upstaged by the boxes they're presented in.

Special parties can be planned, and everything from invitations to table decorations can be perfectly coordinated when you're creating your own designs. Here are a number of ideas to help you plan your own theme parties or wish a friend well on any occasion.

■ **OPPOSITE PAGE:** *This paste paper was made by patterning acrylic-colored paste with a hair pick, a calligraphy pen, and a wooden potter's tool.* **BELOW:** *Gatefold cards with photo centers, cards with cutouts, and other cards created with layers of plain and decorated papers are easy to make.*

■

FOLDED CARDS

Any day can be made to feel like a holiday if you celebrate a friendship with a handmade card. There are lots of ways to fold, cut, and further embellish papers to showcase your paper designs. Cover stock can be scored and folded a quarter of the way in from either edge to produce a gatefold that opens to reveal a decorated center, or if the decoration is on the outside, a message or photograph. Plain cover stock can be folded horizontally or vertically to receive a stencil or decorated panel of paper. Ribbon, gold-and-silver, adhesive-backed mylar, and reflective dots and stickers can be used to enhance paper designs or coordinate with collage work made with sections of various decorated and plain papers.

Thinner papers can be used for cards if they're folded in half lengthwise and folded again in the opposite direction to create a quarto, or French fold, card. This technique gives you a card front that's composed of two layers of paper, which is perfect for making cards with embossing or cut-work on the front. One particularly nice feature is that foils, photos, or other decorated papers can be placed behind windowed areas without being visible on the inside of the card. Most handmade papers are used to best advantage in this format.

Plain commercial card stock can be easily decorated with patterned papers. Just mount your decorated papers to adhesive release paper, cut out strips or simple shapes, and apply them to the purchased blank card.

MAKING ENVELOPES

The easiest way to make a matching envelope for your handmade card is to find a purchased envelope of the appropriate size, steam it open, and trace around it on poster board to make a pattern. You can make an envelope from scratch or from a sheet of decorative paper quite simply, too. Just cut out a sheet of paper that's double the length of your card and equal to the width plus 2 inches (5cm). Lay the card slightly above the center of this sheet, and fold the four sides of the paper around the card. These will be the flaps of the envelope. Next, unfold the flaps, and using the creases as a guide, cut the flaps down slightly to taper them. Then glue the bottom and side flaps in place with a glue stick. You'll glue the top flap down after inserting the card.

If the decorated paper is on the inside of the envelope, it will create a colorful lining. You can also cut a piece of decorated paper slightly smaller than the raised flap and address area of the envelope and tack it in place to line an otherwise plain envelope.

If you're working with purchased envelopes and creating cards to fit them, you can still line the envelopes in a similar fashion.

16-2

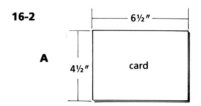

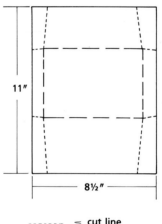

------ = cut line
— — — = fold line

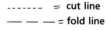

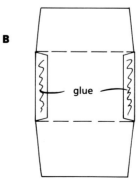

■ **FIGURE 16-2.**
A. *To create an envelope for a card that is 4½ by 6½ inches (11 x 16cm), use this pattern. Cut away the four corner sections, which are bordered by the small dotted lines, and fold the papers on the dashed ones.*
B. *Apply a thin line of glue to the side flaps and fold the bottom flap up to seal it. Insert your card before gluing and sealing the top flap. Modify these directions to create envelopes for cards of various sizes.*

16-1

■ **FIGURE 16-1.** *If you cut a piece of decorated paper to the size of your open envelope and trim it back about ½ inch (1.3cm) all around, you can then coat it with glue and use it to line a purchased envelope.*

■ An oil-marbled puzzle card.

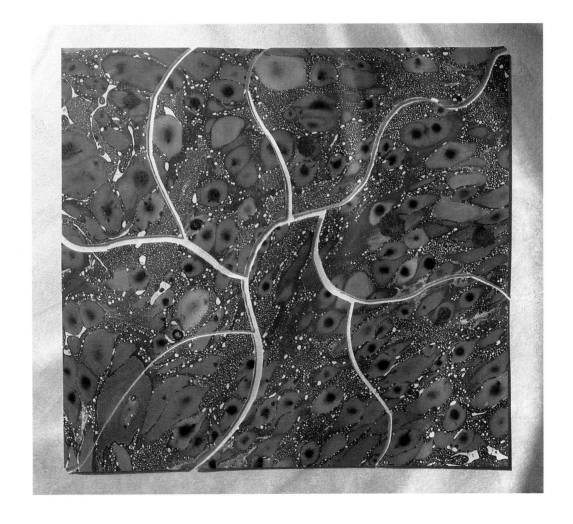

■

PUZZLE CARDS

Puzzle cards can be made from bonded papers. Just mount your paper on a thin mat board, write your greeting, and then cut the card into eight or ten curved pieces with a pair of scissors or a mat knife. Place the pieces in a large addressed envelope (apply extra postage), and mail it to a friend. (You'll probably receive a reply immediately, if only to tell you that your note was puzzling.)

CARDS WITH RELIEF DESIGN

You can let someone know that you're a fan by narrowly pleating a thin strip of paper and mounting it on a card front. Attach the fan folds by gluing the folds together at one end or stitching them together with colorful embroidery floss.

Another way to create a three-dimensional card is to glue mold-pressed handmade paper in place. You might finish the card by adding smooth satin ribbons to contrast with a rough paper texture.

Although cards with attached relief elements may be difficult to send through the mail safely, they are perfect to present in person. That way you can enjoy the recipient's delight, too.

GIFT-BEARING CARDS

A few strategically placed slits or holes can help you create a card that's not only message-bearing, but gift-bearing as well. If you fold a piece of cover stock to create a tall card and make slits near the ends, you can insert a coordinating handmade bookmark.

You can also make a gift pin and attach it to a card front. Just bond a piece of decorated paper to a piece of mat board, and cut out a triangle or other simple shape. Decorate this with beads or bits of shiny paper, coat the piece with acrylic sealer, and glue on a pin back. Similarly decorate a quarto-folded piece of cover stock and punch holes to attach the pin. Such cards can usually make it through the mails unscathed if you write "Please Hand Cancel" on the envelope or use a mailer that is padded.

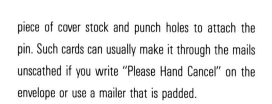

■ *These gift tags, gift box, and medallion ornament were made with oil-marbled and paste papers. Ribbon ties and gold beads were added to make them look especially festive.*

■ **FIGURE 16-3.** *You can enlarge these patterns on a photocopy machine to make boxes of various sizes. Just cut out a pattern, cut on the small dotted lines, and score and fold on the dashed lines. Coat the tab that extends from the right-hand side of each pattern with glue and attach it to the first section of the box. When the joint is dry, you can fold up the box.*

GIFT TAGS AND ORNAMENTS

Delightful gift tags in various shapes and sizes can be created from scraps of decorated paper. You can coordinate tags to match particular gift wrappings or design them so that they can be used as hanging ornaments as well.

To make a medallion ornament, just accordion-fold a long, thin strip of decorative paper and glue the free edges together. Glue the pleated circle to a decorative cover stock, punch a ribbon hole, and add a snappy ribbon tie. Handmade papers cast in a candy mold could also provide gift tag and ornament material.

GIFT BOXES

Festive gift boxes with elaborate decoration are great fun to make. If you add a ribbon loop to a corner of the box, it, too, can be used as an ornament. Some patterns for box designs are located on this page. You can enlarge these to any size you choose by photocopying them.

Box material should be sturdy, so you may want to bond your decorated paper to poster board with spray adhesive or Cello-Mount. Then trace the box design onto your bonded paper. Use an awl or needle to make positioning marks for scoring, then score on the lines indicated and fold up the box.

■ **FIGURE 16-4.** *To make this box (which can also be used as an ornament), enlarge and cut out the pattern. Score and fold on the dashed lines and punch holes to receive the ribbon tie. Fold all flaps toward the center and add the ribbon to gather and close the flaps.*

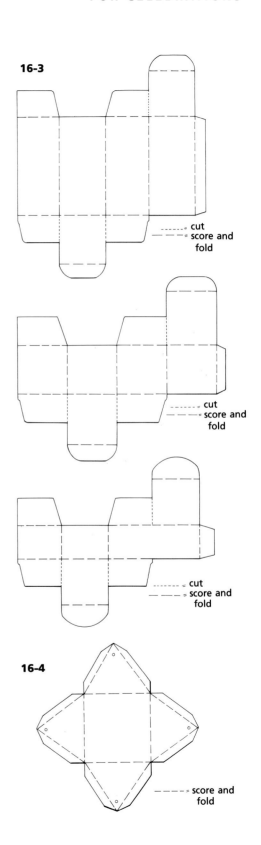

16-3

----- cut
- - - score and fold

----- cut
- - - score and fold

----- cut
- - - score and fold

16-4

- - - score and fold

A GIFT FOLIO

Handmade paper created on a shaped mold or cut from a previously made sheet can be used to carry a gift of several beautiful sheets of paper with messages written on them. The messages could be poems, good wishes contributed by a number of friends, or gift certificates entitling the bearer to gifts of your time—to paint the garage, weed the garden, or baby-sit at some future date.

The pattern for the gift folio is similar to the pattern used to make an envelope (see page 110). The flaps should not be glued, however, and the top and bottom flaps can be more equal in size. Colorful ribbon ties might be added to further decorate it.

PARTY INVITATIONS

Lovely wedding invitations can be made by modifying the directions for the single-signature book (see page 106). You'll only need to fold and stitch three sheets of paper this time: one decorative cover sheet, a sheer endpaper, and an interior message-bearing sheet.

Most photocopy shops can do typesetting, layout, and reproduction for you if you don't want to hand-letter each sheet.

The card pictured is a wedding announcement. To create it, we modified a Celtic-knot design, made a rubber stamp of it, and used gold embossing powder to create a raised design. We glued the paper with the raised knot to marbled paper, and then glued these sheets to a card stock with a recessed panel. Two interior pages were stitched to the card with matching gold thread.

A more informal party invitation can be designed to hold a reply postcard. Simply cut a slit in each corner of your card front and slip the corners of a coordinated reply postcard in. If you stamp and address the postcard, you'll be assured of an early R.S.V.P.

■ *This wedding announcement, made like a single-signature book, is a collage of oil-marbled papers.*

■

PARTY DECORATIONS

You can use your paper-cutting skills to create unique party decorations. For a Christmas party, pure white hanging snowflakes cut in several patterns would be a nice touch suspended from the ceiling on monofilament line of several lengths. For a Mardi Gras party, however, something a bit more flamboyant would be in order. The party garlands pictured were made by folding, cutting, and brush-dyeing a thin strip of rice paper cut from a larger roll. Adding machine tape could also be decorated, folded, and cut to provide a long garland.

■ **ABOVE:** *Snowflakes can easily be cut from rice paper or even typing paper.* **RIGHT:** *These party garlands are over 8 feet (2.4m) long when fully opened. They were dyed with food colors and Pientex dyes and stand 4½ and 2 inches (11 and 5cm) tall.*

PARTY PLACE CARDS

The fan-shaped Mardi Gras place card was made by pleating absorbent paper and gluing it to poster board. The narrow ledge that supports the folded fan was created by cutting and folding back a section of the base board. Narrow slits were made near the bottom of the base in order to accept a changeable nameplate.

To make a place card like this, score and fold a 5- by 6-inch (12.5 x 15cm) piece of poster board in half, giving you a 3- by 5-inch (7.5 x 12.5cm) folded base. Begin the ledge by drawing a 3- by ½-inch (7.5

16-5

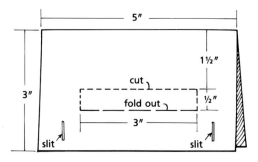

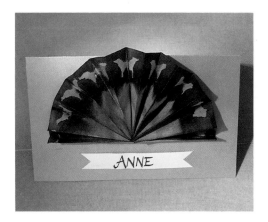

x 1.3cm) rectangle 1 inch (2.5cm) in from either side and 1 inch (2.5cm) up from the bottom of the base. Using a craft knife, cut along the top and sides of the rectangle, then score along the bottom of the rectangle and fold the ledge down.

Prepare the fan by making ½-inch (1.3cm) pleats in a 2- by 13-inch (5- x 32.5cm) strip of paper. You can begin with a piece of decorated paper or use absorbent paper and decorate the fan after it's folded. Glue both ends of the pleated strip over the open ledge to mount the fan.

Now cut two slits near the bottom of the base so you can add a slip of paper with your guest's name on it. Then add some pieces of decorated paper, beads, or ribbons to give the place card some pizzazz.

■ **FIGURE 16-5.** *Cut and fold on the lines indicated to make the ledge that supports the pleated fan.*

■ **LEFT:** *The completed place card with the pleated and dyed fan in place. The removable name plate has been added and tucked under decorative slits in the poster board.* **ABOVE:** *This oil-marbled alligator has removable legs. He can also function as a puzzle and be safely packed away between parties.*

■ *Jennifer Philippoff's amazing beaded mask is designed to be hand-held.*

A style of place card more suitable for a children's party (perhaps following a trip to the zoo) can be made by laminating decorative paper to poster board and cutting out an animal shape. Dinosaurs can also be depicted by tracing or photocopying images from books onto heavy decorated paper. If they're designed to be made in several sections, the place cards can also serve as party favor puzzles.

■

A PARTY MASK

Everyone loves a masquerade party, whether to celebrate Halloween or Mardi Gras, or just for fun. There's an air of excitement and mystery that's unparalleled at other celebrations. Fantastic party masks can be made with any number of paper-decorating techniques; free-form batik and sumi papers or wild orizomegami designs could be bonded to poster board and cut to reveal faces of various characters and creatures.

This mask of a Siamese dancer was made from oil-marbled paper bonded to two-ply mat board. Shiny beads wired in place and a foil-wrapped dowel accent the piece.

Use your paper-cutting skills to design an equally opulent mask. Draw one half of the mask design on a large folded sheet of paper, making sure the eye hole and nose area are in the correct places. Draw and cut the rest of the design with abandon to attain a flowing, symmetrical pattern to trace onto the bonded papers. Add beads, ribbons, or perhaps some pleated fans to add to your mask's flamboyant personality.

$\mathscr{S}$uppliers

■

UNITED STATES

Aido's Art Materials Import, Inc.
714 North Wabash Avenue
Chicago, IL 60611
(312) 943-0745
(*Japanese paper*)

Basic Crafts Co.
1201 Broadway
New York, NY 10001
(212) 670-3516
(*bookbinding supplies*)

Boku Undo, U.S.A., Inc.
594 Broadway
New York, NY 10012
(212) 226-0988
(*Japanese paper, dyes*)

Bookmakers International
6001 66th Avenue
Riverdale, MD 20737
(301) 459-3384
(*bookbinding, papermaking supplies*)

Colophon Book Arts Supply
3046 Hogum Bay Road, NE
Olympia, WA 98506
(206) 459-2940
(*bookbinding, marbling supplies*)

Daniel Smith Inc.
4130 First Avenue South
Seattle, WA 98134
(800) 426-6740
(*art, papermaking supplies*)

Diane Maurer Hand Marbled Papers
Box 78
Spring Mills, PA 16875
(814) 422-8651
(*marbling, paste paper, dye supplies*)

Dick Blick
P.O. Box 1267
Galesburg, IL 61401
(800) 447-8192
(*art, papermaking, binding supplies*)

Johnson Bookbinding Supply Co.
32 Trimountain Avenue
South Range, MI 49963
(906) 487-9522
(*bookbinding supplies*)

Lee S. McDonald, Inc.
P.O. Box 264
Charleston, MA 02129
(617) 242-8825
(*papermaking supplies*)

New York Central Supply Co.
62 Third Avenue
New York, NY 10001
(212) 473-7705
(*art, papermaking supplies*)

Pearl Paint
308 Canal Street
New York, NY 10013
(212) 431-7932
(*art, papermaking supplies*)

Rugg Road Paper & Prints
1 Fitchburg Street B154
Somerville, MA 02143
(617) 666-0007
(*bookbinding, papermaking supplies, paper*)

Talas
213 West 35th Street
New York, NY 10001
(212) 736-7744
(*bookbinding, papermaking supplies*)

Yasutomo
500 Howard Street
San Francisco, CA 94105
(415) 981-4326
(*Japanese paper*)

■

CANADA

Curry's Art Store Ltd.
756 Yonge Street
Toronto, Ontario M4Y 2B9
(416) 967-6666
(*bookbinding supplies, paper*)

E.E. Tigert
95 Nugget Avenue
Scarborough, Ontario
(416) 291-6293
(*art supplies*)

La Papeterie St.-Armand
950 Rue Ottawa
Montreal, Quebec H3C 1S4
(514) 874-4089
(*papermaking supplies, paper*)

Paper-Ya
9 & 10-1666 Johnston Street
Netloft, Granville Island
Vancouver, British Columbia
(*paper*)

$\mathscr{F}$OR CLASSES

Center For Book Arts
626 Broadway
New York, NY 10012
(212) 460-9768

Diane Maurer
Box 78
Spring Mills, PA 16875
(814) 422-8651

Guild of Bookworkers
521 Fifth Avenue
New York, NY 10175
(212) 757-6454

Pyramid Atlantic
6001 66th Avenue
Riverdale, MD 20737
(301) 459-7154

Rugg Road Paper & Prints
1 Fitchburg Street
Somerville, MA 02143
(617) 666-0007

Further Reading

Barrett, Timothy. *Japanese Papermaking.* New York: John Weatherhill Inc., 1986.

Guyot, Don. *Suminagashi: An Introduction to Japanese Marbling.* Seattle: Brass Galley Press, 1988.

Heller, Jules. *Papermaking.* New York: Watson-Guptill Publications, 1978.

Hollander, Annette. *Decorative Papers and Fabrics.* New York: Van Nostrand Reinhold Company, 1971.

Hunter, Dard. *Papermaking: The History and Technique of an Ancient Craft.* New York: Dover Publications, Inc., 1978.

Ikegami, Kojiro. *Japanese Bookbinding.* New York: John Weatherhill Inc., 1986.

Jackson, Paul. *The Encyclopedia of Origami and Papercraft Techniques.* Philadelphia: Running Press, 1991.

Johnson, Pauline. *Creative Bookbinding.* Seattle: University of Washington Press, 1963.

Loring, Rosamond B. *Decorated Book Papers.* Cambridge: Harvard University Press, 1952.

Maurer, Diane, and Paul Maurer. *An Introduction to Carrageenan & Watercolor Marbling.* Centre Hall, PA: Hand Marbled Papers, 1984.

Maurer, Diane Vogel. *Marbling: A Complete Guide to Creating Beautiful Patterned Papers and Fabrics.* New York: Crescent Books, 1991.

Shannon, Faith. *Paper Pleasures.* New York: Weidenfeld & Nicholson, 1987.

Smith, Keith A. *Non-Adhesive Binding: Books Without Paste or Glue.* New York: Sigma Foundation, Inc., 1991.

Toale, Bernard. *The Art of Papermaking.* Massachusetts: Davis Publications Inc., 1983.

_____. *Basic Printmaking Technique.* Massachusetts: Davis Publications, 1991.

Zeier, Franz. *Books, Boxes and Portfolios.* New York: Tab Books, 1990.

Index